CASE STUDIES IN
CULTURAL ANTHROPOLOGY

GENERAL EDITORS
George and Louise Spindler
STANFORD UNIVERSITY

THE NAVAJO

By

JAMES F. DOWNS

University of Hawaii

HOLT, RINEHART AND WINSTON, INC.
NEW YORK   CHICAGO   SAN FRANCISCO   ATLANTA
DALLAS   MONTREAL   TORONTO   LONDON   SYDNEY

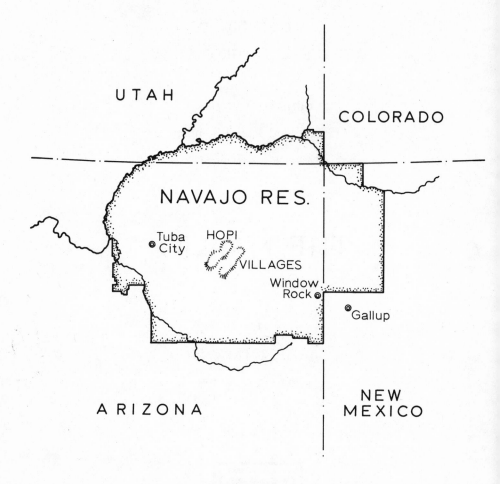

Cover: The owner, in light shirt and hat,
standing, supervises the branding of one
of his calves at the community branding.

Library of Congress Catalog Card Number: 70-173266
ISBN 0-03-085483-0
Printed in the United States of America
7 8 9   059   9 8 7 6 5 4

Foreword

About the Series

These case studies in cultural anthropology are designed to bring to students, in beginning and intermediate courses in the social sciences, insights into the richness and complexity of human life as it is lived in different ways and in different places. They are written by men and women who have lived in the societies they write about and who are professionally trained as observers and interpreters of human behavior. The authors are also teachers, and in writing their books they have kept the students who will read them foremost in their minds. It is our belief that when an understanding of ways of life very different from one's own is gained, abstractions and generalizations about social structure, cultural values, subsistence techniques, and the other universal categories of human social behavior become meaningful.

About the Author

Before becoming an anthropologist, James F. Downs served in the U.S. Navy during World War II and the Korean War, worked as a newsman, professional horseman, and farmer. After conducting field research among the Washo of California and Nevada and the Navajo of Arizona, he received his M.A. and Ph.D. in anthropology at the University of California at Berkeley. He has studied oriental languages and conducted research on Tibetan culture in Northern India in association with R. B. Ekvall, author of *Fields on the Hoof*. He has taught at the University of Rochester, the University of Wyoming, California State College at Los Angeles, and the University of Arizona. He is now a professor of anthropology at Hilo College and the Center for Cross-Cultural Training and Research at the University of Hawaii.

About the Book

The Navajo is a case study of a pastoral community. The author has chosen to focus this book on the pastoral aspects of Nez Ch'ii society and culture, since sheepherding plays a most important role in the history of the Navajo in general and remains the most important focus of the recent culture of Nez Ch'ii. Other important aspects of the culture are described but are, for the most part, treated within the framework of functional relationships existing between the maintenance of the herds and the social and cultural system based on this activity. Although Navajo culture has probably been studied by anthropologists more than that of almost any other American Indian people, the treatment in this case study is unique.

As a background for later materials, the author describes the basic themes of Nez Ch'ii culture, which include the importance of females, the inviolability of the individual, the prestige of age, and the reciprocity principle.

In this study Downs presents a discussion in detail of the relationships between the Nez Ch'ii families and their herds. The family, he writes, *identifies* with the sheep. Whenever any unusual activity with the herd is planned (for example, shearing, or shifting of pastures), the presence of as many members of the family as possible is required. Navajo living at a distance from the family home where the sheep are kept feel the urge periodically to take a trip to "see the sheep" in the same manner that an Anglo might be motivated to visit a favorite relative.

Downs concludes the study with an analysis of the relationship of the people of Nez Ch'ii to the dominant culture surrounding them. The Navajo have been able to adjust to new situations and the Anglo culture without losing their identity. This can be explained in part by the fact that the Navajo are amenable to change in the area of material culture, but many would be considered conservative in their attitudes toward basic changes in the nonmaterial patterns of life. And, as the author writes, the modern situation suggests the need for change far more profound than the substitution of one means of transport for another: ". . . . most of the modern, tribe-wide political institutions that have developed in the past three decades are designed to assist the Navajo in solving twentieth-century problems without the necessity of assimilation into a foreign culture." Downs concludes that "in the final analysis the Navajo must develop a closer relationship to Anglo–American society as a whole."

The treatment of Navajo culture in either its traditional or modern form in this case study is not intended to be complete, nor has Downs attempted to incorporate information on changes over the past few years. Navajo culture and society is very complex, both as a functioning whole and as an adjustive process through time. Further, the people of Nez Ch'ii are not to be considered as representing the whole Navajo population. It is a significant community and one that still holds to the pastoral herding ecology that has characterized some of the Navajo for at least 250 years.

GEORGE AND LOUISE SPINDLER
General Editors

Phlox, Wisconsin
September 1971

Contents

Introduction

SPRAWLING OVER the northeastern corner of Arizona and into the neighboring states of Utah and New Mexico, the Navajo* Indian Reservation covers sixteen million acres, an area the size of West Virginia. One authority has described it as a fifty-first state within the boundaries of three other states. The Navajo tribe in cooperation (and sometimes in conflict) with the United States Government is governed by its own political bodies and maintains its own police force and courts to enforce tribal law. Navajo rangers build roads, dams, and other tribal works and operate a separate park service and tribal highway and works departments.

The citizens of this anomalous political body are the Navajo Indians, members of the largest Indian tribe in the United States. Approximately one hundred thousand Navajo live within the reservation boundaries or on lands immediately adjoining the reservation. Some small colonies are found in New Mexico completely separate from the reservation but still politically part of the tribe. In Los Angeles and in the San Francisco Bay area there are increasing numbers of Navajo who have immigrated to the cities. In the northern plain states of Wyoming and Idaho, semipermanent colonies of Navajo who work in seasonal agriculture have sprung up.

The arid and starkly beautiful scenery of Monument Valley in the northern part of the reservation is familiar to many millions of motion picture viewers as the background for such great films as *Stagecoach*, *She Wore a Yellow Ribbon*, and *Fort Apache*. The same viewers have seen the Navajo themselves appearing in great number in these and other films disguised as Sioux, Comanche, Apache, or some other tribe considered by screen writers to have been more "warlike" than the Navajo. Millions of people have become familiar with the more scenic parts of the

---

* *Navajo* is a word of mysterious origin and is often spelled Navaho. Although there are sound historical, orthographic, and linguistic reasons for this spelling, Navajo is used by the federal government, the Navajo Tribe, and all individuals who have had occasion to write letters to the author. To Westerners, the practice of pronouncing a "j" like an "h" is not disconcerting, and as a courtesy to the Navajo, this spelling is used throughout.

Navajo country through the media of railroad advertisements and post cards. On Highway 66, which passes along the southern boundary of the reservation, hordes of tourists have come into brief contact with the Navajo selling authentic rugs and jewelry and other novelties, often not so authentic.

The Navajo have been studied by anthropologists perhaps more than any other native people in the world. Over the past thirty years there has scarcely been a period when one or more anthropologists have not been engaged in research on one part of the reservation or another. Individual anthropologists have in some cases devoted their entire professional lives to the study of the Navajo way of life. Hundreds of others have cut their professional teeth in the field with the Navajo people. Unfortunately the bulk of this material has found its way into the relative obscurity of the professional journal, and in the main the Navajo people are scarcely known and often badly misunderstood by their closest neighbors, not to mention the mass of American people.

There are dramatic changes taking place on the reservation as communication, education, and economic forces gradually bring the Navajo closer and closer to sharing in the American society. But these changes are relatively new, and for several centuries the Navajo lived a distinct and separate life in high, arid country of the northern Southwest. Their system was well adapted to both the natural and social conditions of the region, and for many years they were the dominant military force in the Southwest and feared neither other Indians nor the Mexican and Anglo newcomers. Despite eventual military defeat of the Navajo, their style of life did not, as is the tragic case in so many Indian tribes, collapse. Instead it adjusted and adapted and expanded into a unique social and cultural system. That system is in large part now outdated, but it had within it the strengths to make even more changes and adjustments without too severely disrupting the tenor of life or the social identity of the individual Navajo.

This book will attempt to describe this special style of life developed by the Navajo in one community. In the more remote areas this life-style continues, and throughout the reservation it forms the foundation on which modern Navajo life is developing.* Much of the data was gathered by the author during 1960 and 1961 when he, his wife, and their son were privileged to live in the Black Mesa area of the reservation. This region was, at that time, remote and isolated and considered one of the most traditional areas in the Navajo country. Information not obtainable by direct observation could be recovered by questioning older men and women who remember, some of them, the first horse-drawn wagon that came into the region. Since then, the author has been able to return twice for shorter periods.

Because sheepherding has played such an important part in the history of the Navajo in general and remains the most important focus of the culture of Nez Ch'ii, the author has chosen to focus this book on the pastoral aspects of Nez Ch'ii society and culture. While the various elements of Navajo life are described, for

---

* The *ethnographic present* is a device developed to present a relatively static picture of a dynamic social situation. The description of Nez Ch'ii society then is a composite of Navajo culture as observed by the author, reported by other anthropologists, and described by older informants.

the most part they are treated within the framework of the ongoing and unending work required to keep sheep and cattle herds and maintain a social and cultural system based on this activity.

Black Mesa is only one part of a vast region with often dramatically different environments and historical circumstances, so the author has also drawn on the great store of research in the Navajo country that has been carried out since the beginning of this century and also on archaeology and historical documents to fill in the background of these remarkable people.

The reader should keep in mind that history never ends and that many changes have occurred since I first went into the Nez Ch'ii country. This book describes life as it was in that place at that time. On this foundation the present— and the future—stand.

To the people of Black Mesa who patiently bore my presence and my questions without fully understanding the reason for either and who gently instructed me to the limits of my ability in the art of being a Navajo, I owe this book, I am forever in their debt. This book is written for my oldest son Chris who with the acceptance of a child went into this far country with his father.

Tuba City
August 1967

1

Evolution of the Navajo People

The Nadene Stock

THREE THOUSAND YEARS AGO—about the time Homer was composing the *Iliad* and the *Odyssey*, five hundred years after the fall of the civilization of the Indus Valley and the rise of civilization in China—a group of Asians separated from their fellows and crossed the Bering Straits into North America.

Some linguists believe that their language was ancestral to a family of Asian languages generally known as Sino–Tibetan. Since their entry into the New World, the immigrants developed a number of languages from the parent stock including Eyak, Tlingit, Haida, and the many variations and dialects of Athapaskan, which includes Navajo. By comparing the number of shared words in these various North American languages and some Asian languages, linguists arrived at the figure of three thousand years ago as a time when these languages were one. This common language, or stock, has been called Nadene.

What caused the Nadene-speaking people of Asia to migrate into the New World is unknown. This was a period of great turmoil in the Old World. All through Eurasia peoples from the interior seem to have been pushing toward the edges of the landmass. Perhaps this migration to the north and east is somehow related to this general situation.

It is difficult, perhaps impossible, to paint even the most brief picture of the physical appearance or the culture of these people. The fact that they were Mongoloids is certain. Dark hair, with very little curl or wave, is one Mongoloid characteristic. Dark eyes are another, and a yellowish brown skin is yet another. Facial characteristics were most probably like those of modern-day populations of Siberia, that is, more angular with narrower lips and more prominent noses than are common in Mongoloid populations farther to the south in Asia. Their babies frequently had, at birth and for several months thereafter, a dark blue pigmentation at the base of the spine, the so-called Mongolian spot, which is relatively rare among Caucasians but almost universal among Mongoloid peoples.

The culture that they brought with them into the New World is even more obscure, made the more so by the many cultural adaptations and adjustments evolved by their descendants. In surveying the known cultures of Nadene-speaking peoples, it is difficult to isolate elements that they may have brought from Asia to the New World from traits that they either borrowed from Indian populations already here or developed independently since their entry into the New World.

Two material culture items that they may have brought with them are the hard-soled moccasin and the strong, complex bow, both of which appear to have Asian origins. Certain elements of their mythology reflect Old World, probably Asian, origins. But this cannot be dwelt upon too heavily because it is a statement that can be made about nearly all American Indian mythologies. Persons who have associated with both Athapaskan, particularly Navajo and Apache, and Central Asian peoples such as Mongolians and Tibetans have often remarked at similarities of attitude and general behavior, but these conclusions are entirely subjective and difficult, if not impossible, to ever establish objectively.

The distribution of Nadene languages suggests that these newcomers, perhaps the last such group to enter the New World before its discovery by Europeans, penetrated or shoved aside a thin line of Eskimo culture along the Arctic Ocean and began to spread out into Alaska and western Canada. Eventually, descendants of this original language were distributed from the shores of Hudson Bay to the Pacific Ocean. In that environmental context, Nadene-speakers adapted to or developed a number of cultural types based either on the hunting of subarctic animals in the tundra and forests of the northwest or on the enormous fish and sea-food resources of the coasts. These latter cultures, called Northwest Coast cultures, are distributed from southern Alaska to northern California and are shared by speakers of languages other than Nadene. They produced one of the most elaborate nonagricultural cultures to be recorded. The latter shared many cultural traits with the Algonkian-speaking peoples of northern Canada and are often listed among the more simple hunting cultures.

Students of North American culture history estimate that the original Nadene language or languages began to diverge from each other about two thousand years ago. On islands off the coast of Alaska and British Columbia two quite divergent groups, the Tlingit and the Haida, developed. The remaining languages are now called Athapaskan and are spread widely but not continuously over western North America.

The Athapaskans

The formation of distinct languages from a common parent stock is a consequence of the separation of peoples. The Haida and the Tlingit, for instance, occupied large islands well away from the coast of North America. Other Nadene-speakers spread east into the tundra and forests, while others moved south. In each of these new groups different language changes occurred, but, in general, they all remained recognizably related one to another.

After the first split-up of Nadene, the Athapaskan languages began to break up as well. Some groups, it is estimated between thirteen and sixteen centuries ago, settled in the extreme north of California where they participated in a form of the Northwest Coast culture, which was much influenced by the cultures of surrounding peoples of California who spoke several different languages. These include the Hupa and the Mattole peoples.

Some time between one thousand and thirteen hundred years ago Athapaskan underwent another schism. A number of peoples split off from the northern and coastal regions and moved into the American Southwest, through what are now the states of Arizona, New Mexico, and eventually Texas and northern Mexico. Although these languages are clearly related to the Northern Athapaskan languages, they have developed distinct enough differences to be given yet another name—Apachean, or Southern Athapaskan.

It is difficult to know what Athapaskan culture was in this period of southern migration or even what the route of the movement was. Some authorities feel that the migration was down the eastern slope of the Rockies. Others feel that it may have been along the western slope. Others cautiously admit that either or both possibilities might be correct and suggest that these wanderers may have come in several waves, or in many small wandering groups, along many routes. As yet, archaeological research yields no evidence that is indisputably Athapaskan in the vast area between Canada and the Southwest. Perhaps we should not expect that it would. Migrant people seldom leave monuments to their passing. And after two thousand years in North America, it is probable that much of the Athapaskan material culture would be shared by many other peoples in similar environments. But even without archaeological support, we can safely assume that the Athapaskans did come into the Southwest and there they developed a number of separate but related cultures and languages.

These newcomers appear not to have been agriculturists. They probably introduced the composite bow into the Southwest and with it the hard-soled moccasin. They may have come as raiders against the farming communities of the pueblo-dwelling people along the upper Rio Grande and elsewhere in the northern Southwest. They may have made a type of pottery characterized by a pointed bottom, but if they did, it was not an exclusive trait of the Athapaskans and was shared by a number of western tribes and perhaps a number of eastern groups as well.

The land into which they moved was peopled by a number of tribes with roots very deep in the area and with connections to the civilization of Meso-America farther to the south. In northeastern New Mexico along the upper reaches of the Rio Grande, the Eastern Pueblo peoples were living in villages, usually located on mesa tops for protection, and farming the bottom lands. Slightly to the west other villages were living basically the same pueblo life but speaking languages known as Keresian and Zuni. In northern Arizona there were, and are, a number of pueblo villages inhabited by Uto–Aztecan-speaking Hopi peoples who share the general patterns of Pueblo culture.

In earlier times these farming Pueblo cultures had been more widely distributed, with outlying communities in Nevada and Kansas and many more communities in the Southwest proper. The earlier communities were not invariably located on a mesa top. The withdrawal of Pueblo peoples into the Southwestern heartland and the movement of villages to easily defensible positions has been considered evidence of invasions of the Athapaskan-speaking peoples. This is not at all clear, however, because there is equally strong evidence that the Athapaskans entered the Southwest after the movement by the Puebloans had been completed.

In addition to the Pueblo people there were, to the west and north, various peoples of Uto–Aztecan and Yuman speech who were not as complex as the Pueblos. The Walapai and Southern Paiute, for instance, were generally hunters and gatherers, although some farming was practiced. On the banks of the Colorado there were Yuman-speaking tribes, noted for their warlike attitudes, who farmed the bottomlands of the river. In southern Arizona the Pima and their close relatives the Papago farmed the arid desert country and lived in villages. Most of these peoples appear to have had long histories of gradual development from hunting and gathering to farming. Crops and techniques suitable to the generally arid Southwest had been invented and developed, and, in general, relations between people were peaceful.

Into this land then came the Athapaskans, hunters rather than gatherers. The Southwest provided them with a stage on which to work out their cultural destiny. The northern Southwest is a variable land with deserts and mountains and almost all the possible environmental zones between these extremes. Inasmuch as the Puebloan peoples tended to exploit the limited areas where farming was successful, the Southwest provided many opportunities for a less sedentary people willing to live more directly off the land. As the environment provided various and different opportunities, the Athapaskans began to develop somewhat divergent styles of life and languages.

Precisely what their relations were with the Pueblo peoples with whom they were in contact, how their society was organized, and how much of their culture was absorbed from their more advanced neighbors we do not really know, but it is at this point that the Athapaskans first appear in history. The early travelers, explorers, and missionaries of Spain met them and gave them a new name—the Apache.

The Apaches

When Coronado probed into the Southwest, he met, east of the Pecos River in what is now Texas and New Mexico, small groups of wandering peoples whom he named the Tayas and the Querechos. These were hunting peoples, moving frequently in pursuit of the bison that lived on the plains in seemingly endless numbers. They may have been newcomers and explorers almost as much as the Spanish. Some authorities feel they entered this region only a few years before the Spanish. It is probable that these were the ancestors of the historic tribe of Lipan Apaches, who adopted the horse and became the southernmost representatives of the buffalo-hunting Plains Indian culture. Another such group, the Kiowa-Apache, an Athapaskan-speaking tribe that allied itself with the Kiowa, may also be a descendant of these early hunters.

Moving toward the west, Spanish explorers discovered the Pueblo people, a great disappointment because the Spaniards had been led to believe they would find great and rich cities. Nearby they made contact with roving people of a much different culture. These too appear to have been Athapaskan-speaking peoples who arrived in the area perhaps as late as 1500, certainly no earlier than A.D. 1000.

Anthropologists and linguists, seeking common elements that might be considered as reflecting the basic culture patterns that Apacheans brought from the north, have made detailed comparisons between the languages and the cultures of Northern and Southern Athapaskans. Such a reconstruction can only be tentative, but, to the degree that such patterns appear to be consistent with the environmental factors and the practices of other hunting and gathering peoples, they are worth considering as a base from which subsequent Southwestern cultures developed.

STYLE OF LIFE

The Apaches live a nomadic life, moving in search of game and plant foods through all the environmental zones of the Southwest. The basic unit of life was a small band of related peoples, probably related to bilateral* rules of descent (although they may have been in part matrilineal and matrilocal, a custom some writers suggest they imported from Asia).

The men, using the powerful sinew-backed bow, hunted the bison, elk, deer, pronghorn antelope, jackrabbits and cottontail, the wild turkey, porcupine, and probably any other game that came their way. Gathering of piñon nuts, grass seeds, berries, roots, and other plant foods was probably the responsibility of the women.

Housing consisted of a conical frame of light poles covered with brush, grass, or whatever else might be handy. Such structures are still to be seen among the modern Apaches in New Mexico and Arizona. Deer, elk, antelope, and buffalo provided skins for clothing, which probably consisted of little more than a skirt or kilt for both sexes plus robes and hard-soled moccasins. Shredded bark was used by the women to make short skirts after the manner of tribes in the Great Basin. They made relatively simple pottery and woven baskets and used the dog as a beast of burden.

Like most hunting and gathering peoples of western America, their religious life was centered on the person of a shaman, that is, a man or woman who was able to receive into his or her body the spirit and power of the supernatural and, while in that condition, to effect cures. The most important ceremony was in all probability that which was held on the occasion of the girl's first menstrual period.

A belief that they appear to have held in common with peoples throughout the northern hemisphere was a special consideration of the bear as a powerful and supernaturally dangerous creature. Beyond this brief sketch we can say little more about the Apacheans at the time of contact with Europeans. Whether, for instance, any of these people had begun to farm after the example of the Pueblos or whether their religion and social organization had begun to feel the impact of the more elaborate systems of the farming people we cannot as yet definitely determine.

---

* A descent system wherein a person reckons members of both his mother's and his father's family as equally related. *Matrilineal* systems are those in which a person reckons his descent in his mother's line. *Matrilocal* refers to the practice of the bridegroom's taking up residence with the bride's family.

DIFFERENTIATION OF GROUPS

However, it was from this basic form that all modern groups of Apaches and the Navajo were to spring. We should, therefore, consider the distribution of these peoples at or about the time of contact. The Pueblo peoples form a very rough and scattered curve that stretches from the upper reaches of the Rio Grande across west central New Mexico and terminates not far from the Grand Canyon in northern Arizona. To the east of them in historic times we find on the plains the Lipan and Kiowa-Apache, to the southeast the Mescalero, and to the immediate north the Jicarilla; directly to the south the Chiricahua and to the west, south of the Little Colorado, the various bands known as the Western Apache. Each of these peoples recognized its kinship with the other, but each was different from the other at least to the degree demanded by the different environments. In addition, the nature of the contact with the Pueblo peoples must also have affected the specific direction that each of these groups took.

This is particularly important in the case of one more group. The tribes mentioned above lived outside the curve of Pueblo peoples. One group, however, occupied the land within that curve and experienced more continued, varied, and intensive contact with the sedentary farming peoples of the area. In any event, the Spanish who established a settlement at Santa Fe in 1609 as well as a number of missions and colonies in the area began to differentiate between Apaches—wild, roaming, hunting, and raiding people who came into their settlements and those of the Pueblo people—and another group, the Navajo Apaches, or Apaches of the big fields.

THE NAVAJO APACHE

In 1630 the Spanish missionary Alonso de Benavides speaks of three kinds of Apaches—the Xila Apaches who lived by the hunt, the Vacquero Apaches of the buffalo herd, and the Navajo Apaches who were farmers. With this later group he had some extensive contact and provides us with our first dependable information on the lives of the people who must have been the ancestors of the modern Navajo.

Navajo, as used by Father Benavides, appears to mean "large cultivated fields." We can say that certainly by 1630 one group of Apachean peoples had learned agriculture from the Pueblos and had begun to adjust their lives to the new means of gaining a livelihood.

These farmers had abandoned their flimsy houses of poles and brush and adopted a semisubterranean house, that is, a hole excavated into the earth to form the walls and then a domed roof formed over it with timber and earth. Such dwellings are found throughout northeastern Asia and were also used in prehistoric times by the ancestors of the Pueblos. In addition to dwellings, the Navajo Apaches built special huts for storing grain.

Men still hunted, and perhaps entire families traveled into the mountains in certain seasons to hunt and gather. The adoption of farming had made it possible to produce enough food to support larger residential units. One consequence of this was the occurrence of polygyny, that is, one man marrying more than one woman. Benavides says they married as many as they could support. As family organization became more complex, so did political organization, and the Navajo Apache appeared to have had a definite feeling of possessing specific territory that they would defend against intruders. The details of their political structure are unknown, but Benavides met and negotiated with a number of men referred to as "captains," apparently the recognized leaders of particular areas.

The Navajo Apache, although very curious about the foreigner's religious ceremonies, were never successfully converted. They had a well-established system of trade with the people of Santa Clara Pueblo, which took the form of "fairs," large-scale visits of Navajo to the pueblos, during which time they traded dressed animal skins and mineral pigments (perhaps even turquoise) used by the Puebloans. That these trading affairs were peaceful seems certain because the Navajo Apaches brought their women and children with them. But all relations between the Pueblo and the Navajo were not peaceful. At least they had a mutually understood means of establishing peace negotiations after hostilities, part of which consisted of the sending of an arrow and some tobacco as a sign of peace.

Archaeological discoveries reveal the remains of Navajo communities from north central New Mexico (1491, 1541) to the Black Mesa region of northern Arizona (1622). However, Benavides' brief sketch gives us the only detailed information we have for nearly a century. Since the Spanish occupation of the Southwest was concentrated in the area of the Pueblos, attention was not regularly drawn to the more remote and mobile Apache groups. In 1680 an Indian rebellion in which both Pueblo and Apache peoples took part drove the Spanish from this region for nearly a decade. During this time there was much intimate contact between the two peoples. Some Puebloans, fearing Spanish reprisal, fled from their homes to live with the Navajo. Much of what we now think of as Navajo culture was born in this time. At any rate, for the period of the early 1700s history and archaeology provide evidence of a people quite distinct from the other Apache groups, a people we can now speak of simply as the Navajo.

The Early Navajo

ECONOMIC LIFE

The Spanish had introduced many new elements into the life of the indigenous peoples of the Southwest. For the Navajo the impact was double because they were absorbing much of the culture of the Pueblos as well. From their Indian neighbors they had learned farming and weaving, borrowed clothing styles and many religious ideas and ceremonies. The most important introduction made by the Spanish was domestic livestock. The Puebloan peoples had also been affected by domestic stock, but they tended to add herds of sheep, goats, cattle, and horses to their already established way of life. The Navajo on the other hand began to shape their lives around herds acquired from the Spanish. The high, arid country of northern New Mexico and Arizona is ideal for grazing sheep, although scarcity of water forces a herder to move rather frequently. This fitted into the roaming existence of the Navajo, who soon combined farming, in favorable locations, with extensive sheepherding. Living in relatively permanent villages or *rancherias* in the winter, they moved from one grazing ground to another through most of the year. Their winter houses were simple but substantial structures of log, stone, and earth, round in shape and often blending completely into the landscape. They are today called *hogans*, a corrupted form of the original Navajo term. In the summer, the Navajo lived in simple brush shelters or huts that were easily abandoned as they followed their herds.

Although they spoke the same language and in large part shared a common culture, there was no political unity among the early Navajo. In each area leaders appeared, informally selected for their wisdom. Their authority appears to have been limited according to the degree of willingness of people to follow their advice. Group activities such as hunting parties, war parties, or ceremonies were directed by men with special ritual knowledge considered necessary for the success of the activity so that power was dispersed among many individuals to be exercised only in specific contexts.

In some areas farming played a more important role in economic life than did herding, but these were considered by the Navajo to be unfortunate situations, and the people living there were said to be poor because they did not have large herds. Because herds of livestock can increase without increasing the demands for labor, many Navajo began to hold very large herds of sheep, goats, and horses. Some of these parcelled out parts of their herds to poor relatives and dependents and thus began to form a distinct upper class of *Ricos*, or "rich men" who had control, through economic ties, over many people. Still the major unit of Navajo life was a cluster of hogans, each housing a married couple and usually belonging to a number of sisters who lived in a matrilineal, matrilocal extended family. This extended family cared for a single herd of sheep made up of the animals of many individual related owners. Individual couples would farm fields sometimes located some distance away from the hogan cluster. Defense and nearness to a domestic water supply and wood for fires all played a part in determining the location of the homestead.

Decisions to shift grazing ground were made on an extended family, rather than a tribal or even district, basis, each group deciding for itself when it seemed best to move. Waterholes and springs were considered common property, but, in practice, the people living and grazing their stock nearby were the actual owners.

By the early 1800s the Navajo were beginning to be known for the long-wearing woolen blankets that were woven by the women and traded to the Puebloan people, the Spanish, and later to the Anglos. Raw wool was also sold and traded, and Navajo men appear to have spent much of their time hunting deer principally for their hides, which were an important item of trade. Women also made pottery that was much ruder than the fine ceramics produced by the Pueblos. Basketry was an old Navajo art, and Navajo baskets were also an important item of trade.

Corn, squash, beans, and watermelon are repeatedly mentioned as Navajo crops, and in some areas peaches were also cultivated.

RAIDS

Besides herding, weaving, hunting, and farming, the Navajo were also dependent on raiding for much of their economic well-being. Warfare was not a matter of honor and glory as it had become on the Great Plains after the advent of the horse. The Navajo were cool-headed, hard-fighting filibusterers who raided the Spanish and the Pueblos and sent parties well into northern Mexico. The Spanish and later the Mexicans sent frequent but seldom successful expeditions against them. The Puebloan peoples alternated between trading and fighting with the Navajo, while the Jicarilla Apache and the Utes to the north frequently raided the Navajo, often at the instigation of the Spanish and later the Mexicans and Americans.

Raiding parties were always formed by a single man calling on his friends and neighbors to join him. A successful war leader had to undergo a prolonged apprenticeship under an older man who knew any one of the several complex war rituals thought necessary for successful operations. Once ordained, a war leader could then call on his friends to launch a raid against some enemy. The most frequent goal was to capture livestock, sheep, and horses in particular. Often going to war on foot, with the expectation of returning mounted, and armed with bows, shields, hide armor and war hats, lances and war clubs, the Navajo were feared by all the people of the Southwest and northern Mexico. In addition to livestock, the Navajo sought slaves, particularly young men and women of enemy peoples and whatever other goods they might find. Enemy prisoners were often adopted immediately and treated as Navajo. Others served in a mild sort of domestic slavery. Still others were sold to the Mexicans and Spanish as slaves. The Navajo were themselves frequently victims of slave raiding and many of them were kept in New Mexico and Mexico proper. It is possible that many of the skills learned by the Navajo were brought to them by escaped slaves returning from the Spanish colonies.

Occasionally, larger war parties were formed to avenge the death of a Navajo at the hands of some enemy. These raids were often composed of many men, but still were entirely voluntary and inspired by individuals. And even when raiding for revenge the Navajo seldom neglected to take livestock, slaves, and movable goods. They never destroyed the economic base of their enemies by burning their homes or fields. One suspects they wished to come back again to harvest the fruits of war.

Although in regular contact with the Spanish and Mexican colonies of New Mexico, the Navajo were in reality just beyond the high water mark of Hispanic colonization. Expeditions, religious and military, did penetrate the Navajo country, but seldom for very long. Observations were sketchy and incomplete. We have no general picture of Navajo domestic life at this time. Polygyny was apparently common for the richer members of the tribe. A man might marry several sisters living together, or he might on the other hand have several wives living in different places that he visited regularly. This latter system, of course, gave a man with in-laws in several areas considerable influence.

Against their enemies, the Navajo, so effective in offense, had little defense. Hogans were located on mesa tops, in little out-of-the-way canyons, or other hard-to-find places. Structures were built so that they blended into the landscape. Lookouts were frequently stationed at high places to watch for the enemy and light warning signal fires if they appeared. But fortification appears to have been an unknown art and withdrawal into inaccessible places the most common defensive tactic.

All the Navajo were not at war with their neighbors. Certain captains and their followers strictly observed treaties made with the Spanish, Mexicans, and, later, the Americans. However, other Navajo did not, and they continued to raid. Unfortunately, the victims of these raids did not distinguish among Navajo, and the peaceful keepers of treaties often found themselves subject to attacks in retaliation for raids they did not conduct.

In 1846, as a result of the Mexican War, New Mexico and much of modern Arizona came under the control of the United States. The Navajo at first saw the newcomers as allies because they had been fighting the Mexicans. They soon learned however that the newcomers frowned upon raids on New Mexican communities or across the border into Mexico. The old pattern of hostilities continued. Some Navajo groups kept the peace. Others readily signed treaties during the periods when farming and herding would keep them busy and broke them when the raiding season began. Nor were the United States punitive expeditions any more successful than had been those of the Spanish or Mexicans. Even though Fort Defiance was established in what was virtually the heart of the Navajo country, the Indians remained powerful and independent. From 1846 to 1860 Navajo raiders stole nearly a half million head of livestock from the New Mexican colonies. It is interesting that when finally defeated the Navajo possessed most of these animals, which they kept in herds and tended. The other Apache bands had stolen nearly as many animals during the same period, but apparently had eaten them as they took them, since they had virtually no livestock when they were defeated.

THE CAMPAIGN AGAINST THE NAVAJO

The American Civil War provided a period of rest for many tribes on the frontier, as troops were withdrawn for fighting in the East. Not so the Southwest. The Union and the Confederacy contended for the area, and the presence of hostile Indians was a threat to both sides. As the early Confederate threat to the Southwest disappeared, local federal commanders found themselves with large forces of volunteers on their hands and no way to utilize them against the Southerners. Rather than see their commands melt away, as volunteer troops were so apt to do, a large-scale campaign was mounted against both Apache and Navajo.

Kit Carson, an illiterate but capable man who had explored the West with Fremont, lived as a mountain man in the days of the fur trade, pioneered on the freight routes into the Southwest, served as United States Indian Agent in New Mexico, was commissioned a Lieutenant Colonel under General Carleton and ordered to plan a campaign against the Navajo. Carson was friendly to the Ute, having once been married to a Ute woman, and enlisting their aid along with that of the Jicarilla Apache, he marched with the mixed force of volunteers, Indians, and regulars into the Navajo country. Too wise to attempt to force a pitched battle,

Carson attacked the economic base of Navajo life. Wherever his command rode, they burned cornfields, slaughtered livestock, cut down peach trees, and in short established a prototype for Sherman's famous March to the Sea. Finally the Navajo, starving and unable to grow food, withdrew into the almost impenetrable reaches of Canyon DeChelle in eastern Arizona. Here for a while they held out, but starvation did what battles could not, and they were forced to surrender. Beyond the high escarpment of Black Mesa in northern Arizona and in the western part of Navajo country, many bands were scarcely aware of the campaign and remained free during the next four years.

In 1863 the Navajo who had surrendered were taken to Fort Sumner at Bosque Redondo, New Mexico. Here the army hoped to get the Navajo to settle down and take up sedentary farming. The plan was a humanitarian one, but it was doomed by bad planning, the weather, and the determination of the Navajo not to be forced into settled life.

During the next four years the Navajo suffered a great deal. Even when they followed the army's directions and planted crops, bad weather ruined them. They were raided by the Comanche from Texas and raided them in return. An attempt to contain the Navajo with a band of Mescalero Apaches resulted in hostilities. Finally, what had been an ambitious and well-meaning plan collapsed, and the Navajo leaders requested that they be allowed to take their people back to their homelands. In 1868 the United States Government set aside roughly one million acres centered on Canyon DeChelle as a reservation for the Navajo, and the people began to return. By this time the captive Indians had virtually no horses, and the trip was made on foot. In Navajo tradition, it is referred to as the Long Walk. To help support the newly freed people, the government made grants of seed, farm implements, and livestock and actively encouraged the Navajo to become self-sufficient rather than dependent on the government for food, as were an increasing number of tribes on the Great Plains. Arrangements were made for supervision and the building of schools. In this latter case, the government was not quick to make good its promise, nor were the Navajo eager to take advantage of education.

GRADUAL CHANGE

Reuniting with their fellows who had remained free, the Navajo began to reconstitute their lives. Despite the sufferings at Fort Sumner, they had learned many things and began to incorporate much of this into their culture. In the matter of clothing, for instance, the Navajo had gone to Fort Sumner wearing clothing styles heavily influenced by both the Spanish and the Pueblo. Women wore dresses made of two blankets joined at the shoulders and gathered at the waist with a sash much like Pueblo women. Men wore short, split-legged trousers made of buckskin following a Spanish style. They generally were bare above the waist and wore a kind of cloth turban or a skin or fur cap decorated with shells, beads, or feathers. At Fort Sumner they had to depend on gifts of unbleached muslin or cast-off Anglo clothing. Using these styles as models, women began to wear long wide skirts with a shirtwaist which soon came to be made of velvet or velveteen. Men adopted the shirtwaist and combined it with long muslin trousers. Increasingly the turban gave way to felt hats for men, although both sexes retained moccasins. Old style Indian saddles gave way to handmade copies of army cavalry saddles. Many items of food and styles of cooking were learned by the Navajo and incorporated into their lives. Most importantly, their defeat had caused them to realize that the power of the Anglo newcomer was such that they could never again hope to live by warfare. With a few minor exceptions, raiding parties were a thing of the past, and armed resistance to the Anglos was considered impossible.

But there were other ways to resist. The Navajo country was not particularly appealing to Anglos, and there was little pressure from settlers. The Navajo could remain in isolation. Living off their herds, they were able to move if they felt the need. With tens of millions of dry, sparsely occupied acres to the west, the Navajo were able to remain in virtual isolation for the next sixty years. Their own industry produced the things white men wanted from the region: raw, wool, hides, rugs, livestock, and silver jewelry. Through the medium of traders, the Navajo could produce these things and in return obtain manufactured goods from the outside world with a minimum of direct involvement. No longer fearing raids from the Jicarilla or Utes, they could devote themselves even more wholeheartedly to the acquisition of wealth, and this they, in contrast to other Indian tribes, did.

Population increased from perhaps twelve to fifteen thousand in 1868 to nearly fifty thousand in the 1930s. From a handful of sheep and goats given to them in 1868, the Navajo increased their livestock holdings to well over a million head. Safe from excessive Anglo pressure in an area without roads or lines of communication, they expanded and developed what the Navajo have come to think of as the true old style of life. Until Arizona's entrance into the Union as a state prevented further expansion, the reservation was repeatedly increased from one to sixteen million acres in size and formed the foundation for the development of modern Navajo culture.

2

Primary Organization
and Physical Environment

The Reservation

ALTHOUGH NOT ALL NAVAJO today live on the reservation, nor have they
ever done so, the reservation is the heartland of Navajo life. It constitutes the environmental and political stage on which Navajo culture
has developed and is developing.

In American history and political life, the term *Indian reservation* has many
meanings. An Indian reservation may be only a few acres of land deeded to an
Indian family or band. It may be an area of contiguous plots of land owned by
individual Indians, or it may be, as is the case of the Navajo Reservation, a large
area with distinct boundaries controlled jointly by the tribal and federal governments. In some cases an Indian reservation is an integral part of the state in which
it is located, with state and local laws applying to the Indians as well as to their
Anglo neighbors. In yet other cases a mixture of tribal laws, local law, and federal
law applies. This confusing situation is a result of shifting policies of the United
States government toward Indian populations.

EARLY HISTORY

Prior to the 1870s Indian tribes, however vaguely defined, were considered as "domestic and dependent nations," sovereign in their control of certain
lands and the application of custom or law. Their relations with the United States
were directed by treaties which, more often than not, were violated or unilaterally
abrogated by the government. After the 1870s Indians were considered wards of
the government, and most of them lived on assigned reservations under the direct
administration of the government. In the 1880s an attempt to detribalize and thus

encourage assimilation led Congress to pass a law popularly known as the Allotment Act. Under the terms of this law, lands held by the federal government for Indians were to be parcelled out to individual Indians to hold in fee simple. The result was that in many cases, after individuals had received their allotments, great areas of unassigned surplus land reverted to the government to be opened for homesteading or put to other uses. Many Indians, entirely unacquainted with the concept of land ownership, sold their allotments for little or nothing and were left landless and destitute. Some authorities feel the entire allotment procedure was a cynical scheme to satisfy land-hungry settlers and speculators who resented the large Indian holdings. Others see it as a visionary dream gone wrong. Whatever the motivations, the results were that over the next several decades, millions of acres were taken from Indian control. Fortunately for many Indians, including the Navajo, the provisions of the Allotment Act were not applied, and they retained their reservations.

The administration of the Navajo Reservation has gone through many convolutions in the past ninety-eight years. At times the entire area was administered by a single agency staff; at other times it was divided into five or more separate agencies, each independent of the other. In the 1880s, with little planning or foresight, an area that was also claimed by the Navajo was set aside for the Hopi tribe; this led to a still unresolved dispute.

CURRENT ORGANIZATION

Today the Navajo Reservation is administered by a superintendent appointed by the Commissioner of Indian Affairs, himself a presidential appointee, under the Secretary of the Interior. The Bureau of Indian Affairs has overall responsibility for Indian reservations, although for nearly a decade the Public Health Service has assumed responsibility for Indian health. In addition to the Bureau of Indian Affairs (BIA), the Navajo tribe itself has gradually developed a political structure and has increasingly taken over the day-to-day management of reservation affairs. Federal law, enforced by tribal and federal policemen, obtains on the reservation. Major crimes are tried in federal courts. Minor crimes and misdemeanors are defined by tribal law and administered in special tribal courts. As citizens of Arizona, New Mexico, and Utah, the Navajo vote in the elections held in these states, not without some objection and resentment on the part of their Anglo neighbors. In Arizona various counties claim parts of the reservation, and a recent voter registration drive has revealed that a substantial majority of the people eligible to vote in those counties are Navajo who live on the reservation and thus are immune from the laws of the county which they might, theoretically, some day control. These many layers of government authority and anomalies of jurisdiction are relatively new. Over most of the reservation's history, the day-to-day life of the Navajo was only peripherally affected by such things. They lived and worked far beyond the end of the paved highway or the telephone and telegraph lines. Their connection with American society in general was tenuous and second-hand. Their attention was devoted not to the reservation as a political unit, but the reservation as land.

The Land

MYTHOLOGICAL SIGNIFICANCE

The wanderings of the Nadene-speaking peoples and Athapaskans through Asia and western North America are obscured in allegory in Navajo mythology that speaks, as do other Indian origin myths, of previous subterranean worlds in which people lived before emerging finally onto the surface of the world. Scattered legendary references to clothing and food habits suggest a past somewhere in the Great Basin, but little else. However, the coming of the northerners into the Southwest and the gradual separation of the Navajo from their Apache relatives is colorfully recorded in the elaborate mythology, which provides a charter for modern Navajo society and cultural patterns. The scene of the miraculous events from which Navajo society is felt to have evolved is *Dinetlah*, "the land of the People." *Dine* is the term used by the Navajo to refer to themselves and means roughly "The People," as contrasted to all other peoples who are, in all candor, somewhat less than acceptable in Navajo eyes. *Dinetlah* corresponds only in part to the present boundaries of the reservation. In earlier times, Navajo life was centered to the east and north in the valleys of the upper San Juan River. It extended—or, more precisely, extends—from there almost to the Grand Canyon along the Colorado line and the course of the Colorado River above the Grand Canyon. In the Southwest, the San Francisco Peaks near Flagstaff, Arizona, mark one of the corners of Navajo country. To the southeast, Mt. Taylor, New Mexico, marks another limit. Each of the corners and hundreds of peaks, mesas, creeks, springs, and other natural features of these areas are considered at least semisacred and are woven into the infinitely varied mythology of the Navajo. Within these confines the sacred curing ceremonies or "sings" are potent. Sacred minerals, salt, paints, and other materials can be obtained only within these boundaries. Although the reservation constitutes perhaps less than half of the ancient Navajo country, the Navajo have never given up the feeling that despite its occupation by foreigners, this land is essentially their own. Families and communities, holding lands under allotment as homesteaders or simply as squatters on large unoccupied railroad holdings, have continued to exist outside the reservation. Travel within these boundaries is relatively safe, easy, and familiar. Outside these boundaries is the dangerous land of foreigners where a person cannot call up the protection of traditional Navajo ceremony for security.

GEOGRAPHY

In general, the land is high, ranging from three thousand feet above sea level to nine thousand feet in the mountains in the center and west of the present reservation. Another condition which holds in all but a few favored spots is aridity. With the exception of the pine-covered mountain ranges, precipitation seldom exceeds ten inches a year and in many places is often considerably less. In the northwest and southwest the land is exceedingly dry, verging almost on true desert, marked only by small oases formed around springs or small rivers that sometimes are totally dry on the surface, although subsurface water serves to support cottonwoods and willows. Much of the country is marked by flat valleys studded with abrupt flat-topped mesas or dramatically shaped rock spires. The central portion of the reservation is often less scenic than the rest of the area, although more productive as range land. A general pattern of ridges, mesas, or low mountains separating long north–south running valleys dominates the geography. In the middle of each valley is a wash where the spring run-off from melting snow and the surprising floods of water that occur during summer cloudbursts drain. Such washes are often filled in little more than minutes and funnel off enormous amounts of water before it has a chance to sink into the soil. In low·points of the valleys enough ground water accumulates to assure the production of crops; in other areas small flood plains or the apparently dry beds of seasonal rivers also serve as fields.

A typical area could be described as a valley that varies from three to five miles wide and is bordered by ranges of low mesas and mountains. Sloping gradually away from the deep-cut line of the central wash, the valley bottom is nearly flat and is covered with sage, greasewood, and numerous grasses. Here and there in the valley are spots of brilliant green where ground water settles, supporting lush crops of tumbleweed before it dries and begins its windblown seeding journey. From such plots there frequently spring cottonwoods or elms growing tall and straight with little limb development. Low, rocky hills may boast tiny micro-oases growing around miniscule springs. The hills and mesas rise out of a gradual alluvial fan which supports increasingly robust plant life and eventually relatively heavy groves of juniper trees before the rock walls rise straight up. In small box canyons and declivities in the mesa walls, numerous springs, often feeding into shallow caves, support small growths of willows and cottonwoods. On the mesa tops, juniper groves crowd out all other competing plant life. A dirt road or wandering wagon track usually parallels the route of the wash, and old-fashioned wind-driven water pumps, often broken and inoperable, mark the efforts of the Navajo tribe and the federal government to improve the water supply. To the traveler, the area appears without human habitation or inhabitants, but an alert traveler will notice networks of sheep trails which converge on small clusters of hogans, eight-sided structures built of mud-chinked logs and roofed with a dome of red–tan earth, or log cabins often plastered with mud and roofed with tar paper. The building materials and lack of any noticeable development near the homesite, save for a brush ramada (a kind of arbor) and a sheep pen made of juniper limbs, make these homesteads virtually blend into the landscape.

3

Society

SOMEWHERE IN SUCH A VALLEY as was described in the previous chapter the road will lead to what amounts to the center of a widely dispersed and ill-defined community: the trading post. On the edges of the reservation these enterprises may have been replaced by supermarkets, but in the interior they are often reminiscent of western motion pictures—a stone or adobe building with a windmill towering over it and a collection of pens and corrals surrounding it. Perhaps a Bureau of Indian Affairs school, a small post office building, a Protestant or Catholic mission building, often both, and the hogans and cabins of Navajo working for the trader, the school, or the missionary form the miniscule town. In some areas a modernistic chapter house where the people of the district meet with their representative on the tribal council adds a touch of the twentieth century. In other places a brush ramada serves this purpose. Here the people living in one or two million acres come to shop, sell their sheep, consult the doctor on his weekly visit, vote on tribal elections, and learn the newest programs and rules of the tribe or the government. Beyond this nucleus the community is composed of the isolated independent homesteads. Such a community is Nez Ch'ii.* It is typical of Navajo communities, retaining much of the flavor of the traditional past and yet possessing details which distinguish it from other communities on the reservation.

The concentration of buildings, people, and institutions that forms Nez Ch'ii is a new element of Navajo culture and society. Each building and the people working inside it represent a link with the nontribal world—the manufacturing centers of America, the federal government, the relatively new tribal government, and the health services—or, through the school, with American culture in general. Each supplies a need which has become important, even essential, to the continuation of Navajo life. But they represent developments less than a century old to which Navajo culture has made only partial adjustments.

---

* *Nez Ch'ii*, in keeping with common social science practice, is a fictitious name used to protect the identity of the individuals who so graciously cooperated with my investigations.

21

To the individual Navajo, traditional social institutions and forms play a more important role. These institutions take the form of the tribal society, a network of kinship and customary relationships centered in people rather than places.

Definition of the Navajo social structure has often frustrated anthropologists because it is so flexible. Having survived enormous changes through the past several centuries and able to adapt to a wide variety of environments, Navajo society has developed almost endless alternatives. However, certain tendencies or themes guide the choices made by the individual who lives in Nez Ch'ii or any other part of the reservation.

The Female Principle

In the nineteenth century, anthropologists postulated that one of the earlier forms of society was the matriarchy, that is, a society dominated by women. Today we are quite certain that no such society ever, as imagined by social theorists, existed. However the expanding ethnographic record has shown us that in many societies the role of women is quite different from that in American, western European, and Far Eastern civilizations.

Ideally, patriarchy can be defined as a condition in which the authority for all decisions is vested in the male. Among males the authority is vested in the father or his social equivalent, and in nonkinship areas of life the relationship of superior–inferior is viewed as a father–child relationship. The opposite of this, then, logically is matriarchy, a condition in which the authority for all decisions is vested in the female and where in nonkinship areas of life the relationship between superior and inferior is viewed as a mother–child relationship. Obviously neither of these conditions ever exists. Even in the most male-dominated societies certain areas are considered the exclusive domain of women in which the female has the authority to make decisions and take action without reference to, or in spite of, the male. Conversely, no society exists or ever appears to have existed in which women have had such an overriding domination of life. However, if these ideal types are placed at the extremes of a continuum and various societies placed between them, we could develop a gradation of social types based on the varying importance of the male and female in the total social picture. On such a continuum Navajo society would fall toward the matriarchal end of the scale; in almost all spheres of activity the principle of the importance of the female is expressed. Children, by and large, consider themselves as part of the descent group of their mother. There is a general tendency to want to live with one's mother after marriage, but more often than not the wife's desire to live with her mother overrides the husband's desire to remain with his. The relationship between brother and sister is important and often may override the relationship between husband and wife. One's sibling's children play almost as important a role in one's life as do one's own children, and the children of a sister are more important than the children of a brother.

The importance of the female and of relationships traced through the female line is constantly reinforced by the use of kin terms in daily life. Any woman, for instance, is privileged to greet any man of whatever age as *shiyaazh* ("my son").

In turn, any man can call any woman *shima* or *shima yaazhi* ("my mother" or "my mother's sister"—literally, "little mother"). However, were he to refer to any boy or man save his own sons as *shiye* ("male form of my son") it would at the best be in extremely bad taste and might well be considered as a grievous insult. When men greet each other, they have a choice of two terms, *shichee* ("maternal grandfather") or *shinali* ("paternal grandfather"); the former is always accorded to those with whom they have the closest relationship or to whom they wish to show the greatest respect. In addressing children, men frequently say *sitsoi*, which means "child of my daughter."

In Navajo mythology the most important figure is that of Changing Woman, who gave birth to the twin heroes who gained much of what the Navajo consider to be their special culture. In daily life the important social units, as we shall see, are those centering around a core of women—mother, daughters, sisters, and their sons and brothers. Affinal relatives* (usually husbands and sons-in-law) play an important but peripheral role.

Although most political roles are carried out by men, political action is not exclusively a male prerogative, and the individual is usually viewed as representing either his mother's family or that of his wife. In earlier times even warfare was not the exclusive prerogative of males, and there are relatively reliable traditional reports of women who became warriors.

Women are privy to religious and magical lore and can become practitioners. In the relationships between the sexes, women are often the instigators, as symbolized in the selection of dance partners by girls in the Squaw Dance and in the control over courting behavior exhibited by girls and women. In the words of a sixteen-year-old high school student when questioned about the selection of partners at an Anglo-style dance, "Well, sometimes the boys ask the girls but . . . in Navajo it's always the girl's choice." This same girl, who was suffering from being hit on the head with a rock by a boy attempting to avoid her attentions, was asked why she didn't let the boys chase her; her reply was that it had never occurred to her. This principle of girl's choice may well have a bearing on the remarkably low occurrence of rape on the Navajo Reservation, which is 9.7 per 100,000 of population as contrasted with 13.7 of general American rural population, although the Navajo average for murder, manslaughter, and aggravated assault is somewhat higher than the general rural average (Young, 1958:p. 139).

The discussion above should not be construed to mean that there is no division of labor along sexual lines, because of course there is. However, the opinions of women as to how and when work is to be performed is considered important and in many instances is *the* important factor in directing the activity of Nez Ch'ii society.

Although it would appear that this theme is an overriding one in Navajo society, we must expect its expression to vary and to be affected by any number of exigencies of day-to-day life, and so it is. Every individual does not consider himself a descendant of his mother's descent line, nor does every marriage result in the establishment of a new household near the bride's mother. Nor is it possible to

---

* Relatives by marriage.

assume that a man—brother, husband, or son-in-law—will in every case defer to the wishes of the women with whom he associates. Such departures, however, are variations on a theme, are recognized as such, and must be justified in practical terms if they are not to draw social criticism of some kind.

The Inviolability of the Individual

The importance of the network of kin ties that is essential to individual survival is balanced by another theme that is singularly important to the Navajo. Despite close and absolutely essential familial ties, the Navajo remain highly individualistic people. Their primary social premise might be said to be that no person has the right to speak for or to direct the actions of another. This attitude creates specific cultural and social responses. In childhood it permits, or rather enforces, the pattern of light discipline by persuasion, ridicule, or shaming in opposition to corporal punishment or coercion. Children, in a very broad sense, might be said to be herded rather than led by adults, inasmuch as adults tend to interpose themselves or some other object between the child and what it has set out to do, thus diverting it from an undesirable activity. The decision of a four-year-old that he stay home from, or go to, a Squaw Dance or to the store with the family is invariably honored, unless acquiescence is manifestly impossible. Often, adult plans are rearranged so that the child can stay home. Perhaps some extracts from my field diary will illustrate:

June 13
  Ben and Maggie Yazzie Yaz went to the Squaw Dance at the Roan Horse homestead. Remained all night leaving Timmie, the youngest son (4 years), in the charge of Maggie's sister. Decided to go to Roan Horse's place on the following day. When we got into the car Timmie came running up and demanded a ride. Maggie's sister shrugged when we asked if it was all right and said, "If he wants to."
  We stayed at Roan Horse's several hours. Through that time Timmie remained with us and played with Chris (our son) and other children. When we got ready to go he refused to get back in the car and shouted and cried that he wanted to stay with his parents. Although Maggie and Ben had clearly not wanted to take care of a child and preferred to devote themselves to card playing, they simply shrugged when we (expecting them to order him to return with us) told them Timmie wouldn't come and said, "It's O.K. if he wants to stay." They were clearly put out because we had been so stupid as to bring him in the first place.

In seven months' close association with seven nuclear families with a total of twenty-nine children below fifteen years of age, I observed a child struck on only four occasions. Only one of these chastisements, I might add, was for disobedience. All the blows involved were rather mild, even when compared with the spankings of the most "progressive" Anglo mother. Disobedient children are often threatened that an uncle or older brother will be requested to spank them.
  Among adults this emphasis on individualism manifests itself in an unwillingness to make a statement that could be considered a commitment of another

person. One learns quickly to phrase questions about other people so that an answer can be given by the informant without violating this rule. Brothers and sisters politely refuse to discuss the others' likes and dislikes, or husbands profess complete ignorance of whether or not their wives want to attend a Squaw Dance. This gives an outsider a first impression that the Navajo know very little about one another, an impression that later is seen to be manifestly false. It is simply a violation of Navajo mores to express an opinion for someone else.

The right of an individual to do as he wishes and to make up his mind creates what appears to an outsider to be a lack of concern about time. For instance, a Navajo may desire to see another about the purchase of hay, to request help in building a house, or to demand repayment of a debt. No matter how urgent the matter may be, there is a reluctance to press the issue or seek a confrontation. The person in question will speak repeatedly over a period of weeks about wanting to see such and such a person and his reasons for wanting to see him. He may even make a trip to see his friend in the hope that he might be home, but seldom would he make arrangements that would bind the other person to a definite meeting place at a definite time.

This individualism manifests itself in political activity to such a point that a council may or may not wait until the chairman is present to begin its business, nor does the chairman feel absolutely compelled to be on time. Moreover, one may, without feeling too much regret, fail to keep an appointment.

Even in the realm of curing and religion, where ceremonial payments must be shared by a large number of relatives, there are no directly coercive methods of enforcing payment. The fear of being accused of witchcraft or of engendering deep and perhaps irreparable family schisms usually enforces participation. When this attitude is confronted with the far more authoritarian and arbitrary attitudes of Anglo law, with its attendant coercive measures, it creates deep and bitter resentments that often manifest themselves in angry and nearly fatal attacks on policemen who must arrest violators, particularly drunks.

In summary, despite the importance of group ties in this area, it should be remembered that the group must and often does make major adjustments to fit the behavior of an individual.

The Primacy of Age

Yet a third theme weaves itself through the structure of Navajo society. That is the prestige of age, particularly age coupled with a life of hard work and the production of many children and grandchildren. Despite the fact that Navajo are very property-conscious and are all, in one way or another, seeking wealth, the possession of wealth does not in itself determine the power structure of the community. Although men of substance are members of chapter councils and make speeches at squaw dances in which they urge practicing good behavior, enrolling children in school, or participating in some tribal or government program, their position seems to be protected as much by their age as by their money. It is clear that old men and women are felt to be repositories of wisdom and should be considered in making decisions. Many young men attend tribal chapter meetings, but it is usually the old men who speak.

Within the homestead group or the nuclear family there is a clear deference to age, from the merest toddler to the oldest matriarch or grandfather. There is no doubt that an old man with a large sheep herd, a great amount of turquoise and silver jewelry, a number of horses, wagons, saddles and blankets, and other manifestations of wealth is an important man who must be listened to and considered when making community-wide decisions. If, however, he has few children or grandchildren, his position will not be as secure as if he were the grandfather (or perhaps the husband of the grandmother) of a large family. Conversely, a man with many descendents, however poor, must be listened to with respect. In part, this must stem from a prereservation time when such a man could count on the armed support of his nephews and grandsons and the husbands of his daughters and nieces. However, even the most destitute old man or woman living on the bounty of distant relatives and without a real family of his or her own is treated with kindness and consideration by those with whom he comes into contact, and should he choose to speak in public he will be heard out with patience and courtesy. His lack of luck and success may suggest that his advice may well not be very good, but his age will assure that his words are heard.

Reciprocity

Another important feature of Navajo society is the view that every debt incurred must be repaid and that the ledger of obligations and favors received should remain in balance. Within the domestic units of the Navajo there is a great deal of sharing, so that the ledger often becomes obscured by the overall obligation to support and assist relatives. Outside the network of kinship or even among kinsmen who are not closely related, *quid pro quo* is the rule. Often this takes the form of what non-Navajo might consider a blatant commercialism. Nonrelatives usually expect to receive money, food, or other recompense for their assistance. This is considered quite normal among the Navajo, who would be loath to accept a favor without making some return. Usually every attempt is made to settle a debt quickly, but, if it cannot be done, obligations are long remembered. Nor are they considered to be only the responsibility of the individual incurring the debt. Should a man be unable to pay a loan or repay a kindness or some important assistance, his relatives often feel obligated to see to it that the debt is paid.

The concern of one family over its debts can be seen in this series of entries in my field diary:

July 25
Drove to Fort Defiance and paid bail bond of Kee Beguey, who was arrested for being drunk at a Squaw Dance two days ago. Another Nez Ch'ii man, Eddie Yazzie, was also in jail. He asked if I would get him out too, which I did. He promised to repay me as soon as he could. Have my doubts, but it is a good investment in rapport.

August 5

Kee Beguey brought me twenty-five dollars, which he said Eddie Yazzie had given me to repay the bail bond debt. Immediately asked me if he might borrow the money. I agreed. Wrong about Eddie Yazzie. He is not working. Must have borrowed the money in order to pay me.

August 20

Two women whom I had never seen rode into camp today and spoke to Agnes. They were clearly talking about me. After they had left, Agnes, smiling at me, said they were Eddie Yazzie's mother and sister, who had ridden over from Signal Point to ask if he had indeed repaid me (must have borrowed from them). Satisfied that he had, they rode home. Signal Point is fifteen to twenty miles to the east. Thirty to forty mile ride to find out if the family debts were honored.

4

The Social Units

BECAUSE THE NAVAJO RESERVATION is large and offers a great many environmental alternatives to which society must adjust and because historical factors, economics, and so on, vary from place to place on the reservation, it is difficult to describe typical social units. However, over much of modern Navajo history the exigencies of a pastoral life have been important in shaping social organization, and it remains thus today in the Nez Ch'ii area, where animal husbandry is important both culturally and economically. The social units described then refer most specifically to the Nez Ch'ii, although the findings and opinions of other students of Navajo society have been included where pertinent.

The Family

The English word *family* is used in two ways among the Navajo of Nez Ch'ii. A man may occasionally refer to his wife and children as his family, but far more frequently his "family" means his mother, brothers, and sisters, and those people descended from them. Thus a man might answer the question, "Do you have any sheep?" by saying, "I run some at my wife's but I don't have any with my family." Similarly, a man living with his wife's parents may say, "I don't know about that. I'll talk to *the* family and tell you tomorrow." Or when asked about a sister's husband, a young man will say (most often with a not too thinly disguised hostility), "Him? No, he ain't no relation. He's just an in-law."

In keeping with anthropological usage I shall refer to the matricentered descent group as the *family*. When speaking of a man, his wife, and his children, I shall use, for lack of a better term, the expression *nuclear unit*.

The nuclear unit, then, consists of a man, his wife, and their, or more properly her, offspring. The tendency for children of dissolved marriages to remain with the mother usually means that most mature wives have children of at least two marriages in their households.

28

It is difficult to make a definitive statement as to which of the partners in a marriage is "head of the house." Clearly the role of the wife in decision making is important, but the husband appears to serve not only as primary wage earner but also as the representative of the nuclear unit outside the circle of immediate kinship. It must be kept in mind that emphasis on the individual in Navajo life colors the marriage relationship. Divorce is simple and the dissolution of marriage appears to create little social dislocation, nor does the justification for such dissolutions have to be great, that is, from the White point of view. Nonetheless, it should be pointed out that many Navajo couples display a great deal of affection for each other and appear genuinely to enjoy each other's company. Moreover, Navajo families become deeply involved in selecting a first husband for a daughter and go to great lengths to prevent divorce. However, should the girl refuse the family's candidate or the young couple reject reconciliation, their desires are accepted. It also appears that a woman's later husbands have less voice in the management of household affairs or economic decisions than do the husbands whom she married when she was young. This situation seems to stem in part from the fact that these later marriages tend to be marriages of mutual convenience for both men and women. Most often the woman has achieved a dominant position in relation to the larger kinship group; she commands, so to speak, several daughters and their husbands and possesses considerable property in her own right. A husband, then, serves to assist in the chores of living and becomes her legitimate sexual partner and representative to the nonkin world. For his part, an older man seeking a wife of mature years, unless he is a widower, may be a bad marriage risk because of connubial restlessness or poor economic position. He then accepts the role of husband with some gratitude, inasmuch as it gives him a share in his wife's herd as well as the general social and economic security stemming from an extended family situation. It should be pointed out here, however, that an unmarried man is not in the uncomfortable position of the bachelor in many other tribal societies. A young man can depend on his mother or unattached sisters for bed and board in return for his contribution to the family labor pool. An old man retains throughout life a claim on the services of his sisters for cooking and shelter, should he not have a wife to provide them. This relationship is clearly symbolized in the traditional responsibility of a man's mother, wife, or sisters for the neatness of his hair when it is worn in the traditional wool-bound queue. The Navajo say that you can tell if a man's wife *or* sisters love him by how neatly his hair is done. An unmarried man's hair is bound by his sisters, a married man's by his wife or sisters. Among more modern Navajo who have given up long hair in favor of the white man's haircut, it is most often a woman who wields the family clippers when her family needs barbering.

One cannot relate the nuclear unit directly to the livestock operation because of the individualism of ownership on the one hand and the wide dispersal of responsibility for maintaining livestock on the other. A husband, his wife, and any of the children may in fact own animals in the family herd. In an informal way, this unit assumes responsibility for its share of the work, but it seldom works as a unit in the sense that father, mother, and children take over a specific part of the livestock operation. More often, all the males take on one job, with the females doing another, while the children help at yet another. Despite this lack of emphasis on the nuclear unit in many phases of Navajo life, it serves as a vehicle for expressing the relationship between the father and his children through the symbolic and real presentation of wealth. Thus, although a man has a clear obligation toward his sister's children, it is not so great as to overrule his responsibility to his own offspring. A Navajo father is expected to give livestock and horses to his children, particularly his sons. A daughter receives a share of her mother's herd and traditionally can expect to remain with her mother's family, but a son, although he shares in his mother's herd, more often than not leaves her family to join his wife's. The livestock given to him by his father does not become part of his mother's herd and thus provides him with portable property of his own that he can leave with his mother's herd or take with him to his wife's family, but which in either case gives him a high degree of independence. It should also be pointed out here that it also permits him to establish, if he wishes, a neolocal household, making him essentially independent of either of his mother's or his wife's family.

Every man is expected to give a horse to his son. Grazing limitations and poverty often make this a difficult gift, but much effort is expended to bestow it, and a number of cultural subterfuges have developed so that the spirit if not the letter of the obligation is observed. It is not uncommon, for instance, for a man to give his only horse to his son, but to continue to use it himself. The obligation was expressed quite clearly by the informant from whom I rented a riding horse and a good saddle. "We're friends, and I'm treating you just like a father treats his son. I'm giving you that horse." The father is also responsible for feeding and clothing his wife and children, a fact that sometimes accounts for the wide range in condition of clothing found among children in the same family. The matter is felt to be entirely the concern of the nuclear unit as opposed to the family.

There is no clear-cut rule of inheritance except that the offspring of an owner have first claim on his herd. In the recent past, the claim of brothers and sisters was considered to have priority over those of the deceased's offspring; a wife, especially a second wife, could expect to receive little from her late husband's estate. In the case of a very old person it is more than likely that actual title to animals would already have been transferred to his offspring or siblings because the oldster no longer could contribute to caring for them. In practice this would mean very little because the older person would continue to be supported from the income of the herd. In this day of small herds it is unlikely that animals would be willed to persons outside the homestead group, for this would break up the herd.

Homestead and Outfit

The most important social unit in the Nez Ch'ii area is a kinship and residence group, locally called an *outfit*. This particularly western American term, referring to a cattle or sheep ranch, has an entirely different connotation among the Navajo and, it would appear, yet another connotation among anthropologists who work with the Navajo.

Kluckhohn (1947: pp. 62, 63) has described the outfit as a unit that is larger than an extended family and bound together by kinship ties and economic cooperation. The outfit is widely dispersed in a territorial sense, a community in its own right with a leader, usually the eldest male but with a matrilineal orientation (Sasaki and Adair [1952: p. 102] define it somewhat differently).

This definition, however, does not entirely apply in the Nez Ch'ii area. When Nez Ch'ii Navajo use the term *outfit*, they are usually referring to a much smaller unit. Essentially they are speaking of an extended family. Such a group is most often composed of a number of related females living close together and sharing the responsibility and benefits of a single sheep herd. The actual location of residences may be extremely compact, several nuclear families living within a hundred yards of each other, or somewhat more dispersed, with nuclear residences spread over perhaps half a mile.

To avoid confusion, I have used the term *homestead group* to describe this unit and *outfit* to describe the larger unit as defined by Kluckhohn. It might be pointed out here that the term *outfit* is unknown on some parts of the reservation, notably the Navajo Mountain area to the north and west of Nez Ch'ii. I suspect that the Nez Ch'ii usage may well be the result of changes in social structure that have taken place in the past two decades and that the outfit, as described by Kluckhohn, did exist in the area until very recently. Older Navajo tend to use the term *outfit* in a way closer to Kluckhohn's definition; younger people tend to say "our relatives."

Today, herds are so small that large-scale cooperation in livestock handling is no longer necessary, and any work on the herd can be carried out by the family, which has gradually taken over the title formerly given to the largest cooperative livestock group. Moreover, the end of warfare has probably reduced the demand for cooperation between related families. The *chapter system* of political organization that is in effect today with its elected tribal delegate and elected chapter council has supplanted informal councils of elders from the various outfits and placed all the chapter-area residents in a common political framework superseding the outfit. The tribal resource-development crews and the district grazing committees have also taken over what were functions of the older outfit. However, more extended sets of interfamilial relationships reveal themselves on social and ceremonial occasions and during communal sheep enterprises. The people who cooperate as hosts at a Squaw Dance are referred to as "relations." At a community sheep dipping, each extended family is usually joined in a casual way by a number of men who assist in driving sheep through the chutes and vat and who are also described as "relations." At least some of the same men appear associated at both events.

The homestead group, however, is clearly functional and easily defined in the Nez Ch'ii area. Most often the group consists of an older woman, her daughters, and perhaps younger sisters. In addition, the group will include the husbands of the married women. Not infrequently, one or more sons of the elder or dominant women will be part of the group together with their wives. The dominant woman may not be the eldest; an old grandmother or aunt may have a dowager position, although no longer able to contribute much labor to the group's maintenance. Essentially, then, this homestead group is a number of nuclear units related to each other by connection to the family of one of the spouses.

Additional and casual members may be relatives of one or more of the husbands or siblings, half-siblings, or cousins of the matrilineal core of the group. There appears to be a tendency for these casual members to be male rather than female.

The homestead group, however, is much more than a living expression of a kinship reckoning system. It might be described as the minimum unit of survival. In fact, it is safe to say that the survival of the nuclear family is impossible unless it has totally abandoned livestock keeping and exists either from subsistence farming or from income derived outside the area.

The homestead group is a residence unit, in addition to a kinship unit. It is not simply a number of related nuclear units living relatively close together and cooperating in certain economic activities. There are several levels of co-operation. (See Spatial Relations 1960–1962 and 1967 for makeup of one homestead.)

COOKING AND KITCHEN KEEPING

In theory, each wife is supposed to cook for her husband and children, which would suggest the existence of separate cooking arrangements for each nuclear unit. This is not the situation, however, and there is a tendency to share cooking responsibilities among several nuclear groups or, more properly, among several related women. The degree to which this is done, of course, varies with the number of nuclear units involved. The homestead I was able to observe most closely, which was occupied by seven nuclear units, generally used three cooking fires. One fire was that of the dominant woman in the group, who cooked for her husband (her third) and her children still living with her, ranging in age from four to seventeen. She was assisted at times by her husband and her eldest un-married daughter, about ten years old. A second cooking fire was shared by the dominant woman's younger sister, a married daughter of the dominant woman, and the wife of her second eldest son. In addition, two teen-age unmarried grand-daughters and a nineteen-year-old unmarried niece assisted their mothers. It was at this fire that the homestead's seventy-year-old grandmother ate and assisted as she was able. This fire was also shared by a second married daughter, whose husband worked off-reservation, and her children. A third fire was maintained at the house of a third daughter, who was currently unmarried but mother of five children, including two adolescent daughters. Her house and fire were shared by her eldest brother and his wife and children when they visited the homestead. In addition, she provided food and housing for her mother's brother, who lived at the homestead about one-half of the time in the summer. This arrangement of cooking fires resulted in a sharing of the kitchen duties by adult women and adolescent daughters.

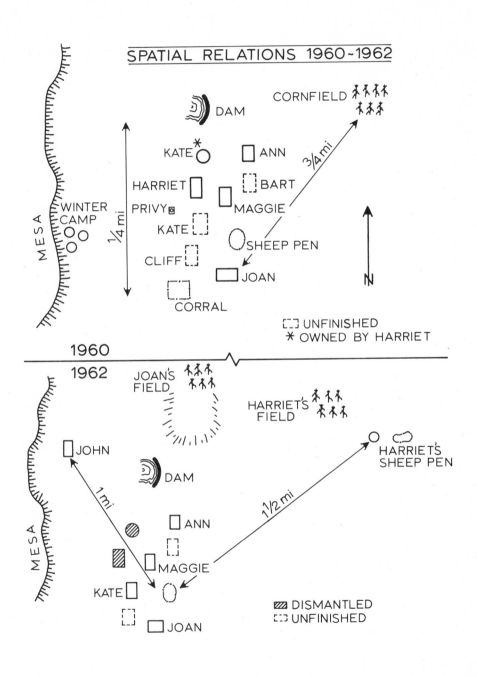

SPATIAL RELATIONS 1960~1962

1960

CORNFIELD

DAM

KATE * ANN

HARRIET BART

PRIVY MAGGIE

KATE

CLIFF

CORRAL

WINTER CAMP

MESA

¼ mi

¾ mi

SHEEP PEN

JOAN

N

⌶ UNFINISHED
✻ OWNED BY HARRIET

1962

JOAN'S FIELD

HARRIET'S FIELD

JOHN

DAM

ANN

MAGGIE

KATE

JOAN

HARRIET'S SHEEP PEN

MESA

1 mi

1½ mi

▨ DISMANTLED
⌶ UNFINISHED

SPATIAL RELATIONS 1967

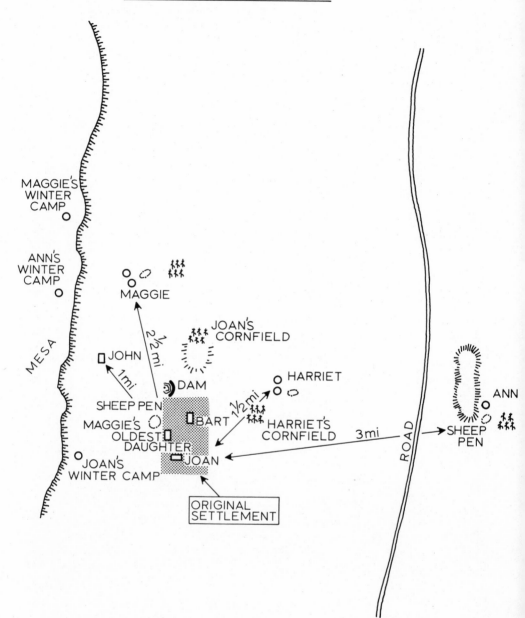

AGRICULTURE

Each homestead has at least one cornfield. In homesteads with more than one cornfield there appears to be a tendency for certain nuclear groups to combine efforts in plowing, planting, cultivating, and harvesting, although the entire homestead group shares in the produce.

WATER AND WOOD

Providing water and wood is the concern of the entire homestead group. Water is drawn from a well or spring in either a wagon or truck by at least two men of the homestead group. The job of getting water devolves on whichever men are available when the supply is low. Water is usually kept in a central location in barrels or tanks and is carried to the various cooking fires as needed.

Wood may be brought into the homesite piecemeal from nearby supplies by one or two women, but it is more often cut in quantity by men. A wagon is driven into the nearby hills and a load of firewood brought back to be dumped in a common woodpile. Keepers of the fires may then drag a log or two closer to their homes and obviate the need for a long walk prior to each meal.

In hauling wood or water there seems to be no patterning of which men work together. Even brothers-in-law who are not fond of each other ride together willingly in these tasks. Younger boys tend to accompany their fathers or older brothers.

SHOPPING

As each nuclear unit has an independent status within the homestead, shopping is carried out independently by the women. However, food tends to be pooled within each cooking group, and a couple seldom go to the trader's by themselves because some other member of the group usually will take advantage of the occasion to hitch a ride.

RITUAL AND CEREMONIES

The most common ritual on a modern homestead is that of the male sweat-lodge. The lodge is usually located some distance from the homesite and, if at all possible, near a water source. Participation is entirely voluntary, but usually at least two members of the group take part, often all the males, including small boys. Men sweat once or twice a week or whenever one of the men of the group feels the need.

The second most regular ceremonial or socioceremonial activity is the summer Squaw Dance. Several homesteads must cooperate to supply the food for the feasting on the first night and the final morning of the three-day event. As suggested earlier, the homestead group joins other similar groups in the joint effort of acting as hosts. These homesteads are related to each other through the matrilineal principle (that is, members of the same clan). They are not, however, the only participating homesteads. Consanguineal or affinal relations of the family of the patient (that is, the person in need of a ritual cure for one reason or another) for whom the dance is given may well come from distant areas to take part.

Within the homestead group the nuclear units each contribute food, money, livestock, and labor to the affair.

CURING

The homestead group operates as a totality whenever one of its members holds a *sing*, or curing session. The patient may be expected to stand a large part of the cost, ranging from five to twenty dollars in cash, a ceremonial basket costing from three to six dollars, and food for the singer during his stay, which varies from one to five days. The rest of the group is expected to assist. More importantly, each member is expected to participate. This requirement binds even the most acculturated, who may openly disparage singing and singers but must attend certain parts of the ritual. At certain times all members of the group, including infants, must be present.

LIVESTOCK

The entire homestead shares the responsibility of and benefits from the sheep herd. Although individuals have title to individual animals, the work is shared and divided along the lines of sex and age rather than in terms of nuclear units.

The following account describes the working arrangements in a single homestead group as it prepared for and finally participated in the annual sheep dipping in mid-August. The animals are dipped in pesticide solution to kill insect pests and prevent mange. Marking was done in mid-July while the herd was penned at midday. Broken Foot, the eldest son of the dominant woman, assisted by his second sister and her children, did the marking job.

Three days before the dipping the entire homestead group assembled at the sheep pen. The job at hand was to attempt to separate the various classes of livestock—adult sheep, lambs, goats, kids, and rams—inside the pen and then move them in single file through the gate. At that time they were counted and the herd reassembled.

The separation in the pen was carried out by adolescents with the help of one or two adults. The actual counting was done by a single person; at first it was one of the adolescent girls who attended high school, but later the second oldest brother took over.

The sheep, already terrified by the separation within the pen, panicked completely at the gate and attempted to surge through en masse to rejoin their fellows. Keeping the stream down to countable proportions required that two adults assist the tallyman at the gate. All adults and adolescents were present, shifting from interested and vocal spectators to active participants, as the occasion demanded. All children able to walk were clumsily involved in herding.

The evening before the dipping day the herd was assembled and driven toward the vat about five miles away by all of the adolescents. The only exceptions

Sheep emerging from the dipping vats in the background. Sheep dipping is a time of homestead cooperation and often a display of clothing and jewelry by the women.

were two oldest girls, who were at that time living with a sister-in-law near the trading post, but who were summarily ordered home to help their mothers. Directing the herding operation was the dominant woman, her husband, her brother-in-law, and one of her adult daughters, who drove the wagon. This group remained camped by the vat during the night. In the morning they were joined by an older brother and a younger son who had not gone on the herding drive. The younger sister of the dominant woman, one daughter, and a daughter-in-law remained at the homesite to watch the youngest children who did not go to the dipping. It was at this point that the adolescent girls were called home to help with the cooking.

The adolescent boys riding the homestead's team drove the sheep home and then rode back to the vat so that the team could haul the wagon back to the homestead.

During the dipping, everyone—adults, adolescents, and children—assisted in holding the herd and separating them for vaccination against disease. When the sheep entered the chute, the men and boys took over the job of driving them and throwing them into the vat assisted by a number of male "relatives." The women and adolescent girls took up the community dipping-poles to move the animals through the vat and to see them into the dripping pen. This last step was supervised by one of the daughters of the dominant woman. The dominant woman had assumed the job of cooking for the entire homestead at a fire built near the wagon.

The Clan

Beyond the family, the outfit, the homestead group, or even the vague concept *relatives*, there is a larger social unit which serves to tie the Navajo together as a people. This is the clan.

Here, too, the female principle is paramount. Each person is considered to be a member of the clan of his mother. Experts differ on how many clans the Navajo people believe exist, but it is certainly more than fifty. Seldom are all clans represented in any one area. But, on the other hand, no area appears to be the exclusive domain of a single clan. Among some tribal peoples, the clan plays a singularly important role governing land tenure, ceremonial activities, and governmental functions. However, such is not the case among the Navajo. There are no clan councils or chiefs. In a given locality the most respected man of a clan may be considered something of a leader by his clan relatives, but in all probability his prestige extends beyond clan boundaries, and his authority, if such it can be called, is territorial rather than kin-based. Often a rather large area will be occupied almost exclusively by homestead groups representing a single clan, but such an area appears to be in fact simply the contiguous grazing lands of homestead groups which consider themselves to be quite independent. This situation develops rather frequently as homestead groups grow too large for efficient grazing and are unable to contain the tensions and frictions of a large number of people living close together. Particularly after the grandmother in such a group dies, there is a tendency for her daughters and their daughters to strike out and set up new homestead sites, thus forming the outfit. The clan affiliation remains unchanged, of course, but each new unit looks upon itself as sovereign. Because sons so frequently bring their wives to live in their maternal home and establish separate households when the break-up occurs, outfits seldom consist entirely of people of the original clan. The children of these daughters-in-law, of course, are members of her clan. The Navajo speak of being "born for" their father's clan and cannot marry these paternal relatives. Their relations to their cousins, then, even if of a different clan, are essentially those of "brothers" and "sisters." Thus, the flexibility of postmarital residence choices, coupled with the dynamics of the transformation of the homestead group into the outfit, precludes control of large areas by members of a single clan.

The clan seems to function largely to determine eligible marriage partners. The rules of the incest taboo extend to any person of the same clan, no matter how distantly related. One is also forbidden to marry a member of his father's clan. In some cases two or more clans, often because of their relationships at the time of their forming, which is recounted in the tribal origin myth, are considered to be related, and their members are forbidden to each other. Some clans practice minor eccentricities such as avoiding certain foods, but this is not the case for all clans. The formation of clans appears to be a process which has been continuous in Navajo society. Some clan names such as Nakai ("Mexican" or "foreigner") and Hopi clearly reflect the incorporation of foreigners into Navajo life. A person's clan affiliation can often be determined by certain idiosyncrasies of word usage or pronunciation.

When a Navajo is traveling in a strange part of the reservation, members of his clan are obliged to provide him with food and shelter if he asks for them. Clan mates are also expected to assist in various ways in ceremonial situations both ritually and financially.

Kinship and Kinsmen

A Navajo living in Nez Ch'ii spends his life among people he considers to be relatives. An informant in his early sixties described his childhood and youth as a period when he seldom saw people his own age save his "brothers" and "sisters." In his youth the land was less full, and homesteads were even more widely dispersed than they are today, but in a very real sense the situation has not changed.

GENERAL BEHAVIORAL GUIDELINES

The principles of social organization that have been described operate along a network of kinship ties, which are defined by kin terms that in themselves define how one person should act toward another in specific situations.

A Navajo is, as we have seen, a member of his mother's clan. This means that all other people of the same clan are considered kinsmen. The Navajo do not maintain complex and detailed genealogies as do some peoples. Rather, they simply classify entire groups of people in one category and apply a suitable term. A man you have never seen before, coming from perhaps a hundred miles away but claiming membership in your clan, is called *brother* or *mother's brother* and treated accordingly. But beyond that, a Navajo was "born for" his father's clan, and thus entire classes of people fall into similar categories because of their relationship to this line of descent. And because clans form the vague and un-named coalitions or linkages mentioned earlier, yet further extensions of kinship can be made along these lines.

The kin term one uses to address another person indicates the way one acts toward that person, how much help one can expect in a crisis, whether they may or may not joke about sexual matters, the degree of authority one may exercise over the other, or indeed whether they can rightfully speak at all.

Of course, this is not a unique characteristic of the Navajo or even of tribal people. All societies use kin terms as guidelines for behavior. The love-sick American boy who is told by a girl that she thinks of him as a brother knows exactly what the young lady means; he is not, in her opinion, a competitor for her sexual favors. Priests are called "father" and nuns "sister" for precisely the same reasons.

Among tribal people, the Navajo included, the principles of kinship are more extensive and pervasive and may constitute the network of communications in which many decisions of a political, economic, or legal nature are made.

David Aberle's discussion of Navajo kinship (Aberle, 1961) sums up the general characteristics of Navajo kin behavior very nicely when he says there are two kinds of relatives: those with whom one is bashful and those with whom one is easy.

My informants did not use these terms, but the description fits very well. What this means is that there are a number of people in each person's life who are dealt with in very polite terms or perhaps approached through intermediaries rather than directly. Others can be approached directly and asked for assistance. These relatives with whom one is easy can also be joked with, often quite obscenely, with propriety.

The most notable bashful relationship is between a man and his wife's mother. Traditionally these two persons could not speak to each other, avoided looking at one another, and usually tried to avoid being in the same room with each other. This practice, which is not unique to the Navajo, is known as the mother-in-law taboo. Most authorities feel it is a way to avoid any possibility of conflict between mother and daughter over the sexual favors of the daughter's husband. However it might also be a simple means of avoiding the kind of son-in-law, mother-in-law relationship which is so much a part of our own domestic folklore. In Nez Ch'ii today, mother-in-law avoidance is gradually dying out. However there still is an air of restraint between these two relatives. In the past, old persons in this relationship could simply agree to give up the avoidance practices. If a man is a singer and must in some emergency sing over his mother-in-law, the avoidance is broken thereafter, and he uses another kin term toward her. And if, as was not uncommon, a man marries an older woman and later marries her daughter from a previous marriage, there is no avoidance requirement. Similarly, if he has sexual intercourse with a woman and later marries her daughter by another man, he does not practice avoidance. In Navajo eyes avoidance behavior is a sign of mutual respect and should be practiced by both parties, although in fact the burden is most often on the man.

Between parents and children there is some difference in behavior of children toward their mother and father. Children will usually approach their mother directly to ask for a favor or for help. However, girls particularly are a bit reluctant to approach their fathers, but rather use their mothers as intermediaries. Fathers and sons have a more direct relationship, one that may include fairly rough joking, which emphasizes the fact that a father and son are of different clans.

Between siblings, age is a great determiner of authority and attitude. The elder generally assumes authority over the younger throughout life, very much (in the case of women) as she did when the younger was a child and the elder assisted in caring for her.

Between brothers, the elder will generally approach the younger directly, and the younger may do the same, but he may ask his sister to act as intermediary. Not infrequently, when a mother or sister wishes to ask a favor of a married son or brother, they first approach his wife. A sister will sometimes have her children ask her brother in her behalf for a favor or for help. This, of course, symbolizes the relationship between a man and his sister's children. He would be much less likely to refuse them than he would his sister.

Although the relationship between siblings is very close, there is also an element of "bashfulness" or restraint between them. Joking about sexual matters is forbidden or handled with extreme delicacy, so circumspectly that an outsider would scarcely know what the subject of the discussion was. Generally a brother and sister never travel together alone, and in the past they were not supposed to hand objects to each other. The closeness of siblings can also be seen in the traditional attitudes toward distribution of a person's property at the time of his death. A man's was distributed, not to his spouse and children, but rather among brothers and sisters. Today, American patterns of inheritance, which are enforced by the courts, are causing much domestic unhappiness among the Navajo, who resent the fact that a spouse and children will inherit more than brothers and sisters.

The importance of women in the Navajo system is illustrated by the fact that a brother or sister often avoids asking a married brother for help directly, preferring to refer to his wife first. This is true when one asks a friend who is not a relative for help. If the friend's wife is present, she must be consulted before the husband can make a commitment.

In matters of authority and allocation of work or wealth the elder usually exercises authority over the younger in the case of siblings. However, a sister has far more extensive claims on a brother than does a brother on a sister. She can ask his help in farming or herding, request and expect gifts of money or food. A brother cannot generally deny these requests, although he can claim that his wife's family made demands that superseded those of his own family. One of Aberle's informants pointed out that in the case of conflicting requests he could hold his own family off by saying that his wife's family wouldn't let him comply. Because one cannot talk to a mother-in-law, one cannot argue or explain save through the intermediary of his wife.

I have mentioned elsewhere some of the obligations a father has toward his sons. In general, his role is one of authority and support. He is required to provide for all his children and to teach them properly. The mother's brother, who plays such an important role in many matrilineal societies, is not so important in Navajo society, unless the father is not present. However, he may be called upon to help discipline children and most certainly has a number of economic and ritual obligations toward them. Traditionally it was he, not the father, who helped arrange marriages, although the father would receive part of the gifts given by the bridegroom to the family of the bride.

Aberle sums up the general pattern of relating to kinsmen in this way:

In general, the communications of consanguine [or what we would call "blood"] kin and of husband and wife are direct and unimpeded. Age and generation differences sometimes produce asymmetrical patterns. Thus the mother is sometimes used as an intermediary when a junior consanguine needs leverage in asking the assistance of senior kin. No intermediary is used for the mother herself. Mother's brother–sister's son relations are handled directly. The direct communication of brother and sister is disrupted by marriage, and particularly by the brother's marriage. Then his wife or his sister's children serve as intermediaries.

A man's communications with both male and female affines are largely indirect, whereas a woman's with female affines are often direct. This asymmetry is not reflected in kinship terminology, it will later be seen. [Aberle, 1961: p. 162]

I have mentioned in passing the matter of joking. Among the Navajo of Nez Ch'ii, as elsewhere, with whom one can joke and what kind of jokes may be employed are determined largely by kinship relationships. Anthropological studies have emphasized this kind of interaction to the point that such patterns are often seen as the unique quality of primitive or tribal people. Of course that is not the case. If we examine our own lives, we will see that we joke with certain people in quite a different way than we do with others. And with some we do not joke at all. Generally we do not joke with parents about sexual matters, but we may well do so with cousins or with friends. The difference between ourselves and the Navajo lies only in the fact that so much more of their social universe is defined by kinship classifications.

A brother and sister may joke with each other, but such bandying must never have a sexual connotation. Either one may make derogatory jokes about the other's appearance or make funny remarks about the other's abilities and skills. Much the same pattern is observed between the children of sisters (that is, parallel cousins). As siblings get married and grow older, the formalities between them become more rigid and approach almost prohibition or avoidance relationship.

Joking with parents must also avoid sexual references and usually refers to membership in clans. A boy can for instance refer to his mother as "woman who married into my father's clan," and thus in a sense speak of her as an in-law (Aberle, 1961: p. 152). Such joking might be called a play on kinship just as we make plays on words. Such references are often a part of Navajo joking and considered a basis for much humor. They bring to mind the humorously intended song of a few decades ago which dealt with the supposed marital habits of hillbillies, I Am My Own Grandpa.

With his mother's brother, however, a young man may joke about sexual matters. Almost no subject seems taboo; genital size, rape, seductions and conquests the other is supposed to have made, as well as plays on their kin relationship, which is complicated by the fact that his mother's brother can marry a woman of his nephew's father's clan—which of course the younger man can not do.

Cross cousins—that is, the children of the mother's brother or of the father's sister are of different clans than are the mother and father's own children, and in fact are eligible mates. Between such relatives joking can be rough and obscene. Male cross cousins, according to Aberle, can make virtually any topic the subject of joking. In addition they may wrestle, race with each other, or in other ways demonstrate a kind of friendly (generally) rivalry between them.

Aberle sums up various styles of joking in this way:

> Members of a clan joke about the things that divide them: different paternal affiliations. Parents and children joke about their different affiliations. Brothers and sisters joke about their different fortunes and their marital ties, if in a rather cautious fashion. Cross cousins, whose affiliations are clearly different, joke about the delicacy of the marriage bond. Outsiders press home jokes centering about a person's paternal affiliations or his siblings'—not his own—in-laws. In-laws do not joke, according to Dapah, although Reichard says that father-in-law and son-in-law do. In general, the non-joking and avoidant relationships create the ties about which the jesting revolves. [Aberle, 1961: pp. 156–157]

KIN TERMS

Many anthropologists have studied Navajo kinship terminology, and generally one must conclude that it is a very complex subject. Not all authorities agree as to precisely what term is applied in what case. This diversity can be attributed to the differing memories of informants or variations among different areas on the reservation and different times during which the field work has been done over nearly half a century. Nonetheless, the main themes and patterns of Navajo kinship terminology can be demonstrated by examining the list below. Each of the items listed is prefixed with the term *shi*, which is best translated as "my," the Navajo having no way to express these names save in personal terms. This is also true of most Navajo nouns, which must be prefixed with a possessive to be intelligible.

CATEGORIES OF NAVAJO KINSHIP

Possessive	Term	Relatives included*
shi	ma	mo, *mosis*†
	ma yazhi	*mo sis*, mosisda, fasisda, elsisda
	ma-sani	momo, mafasis, momosis
	Ch'aii	mofa, mofabro, momobro, *mofabro*
	Nali‡	fafa, famo, famosis, famobro, fafabro, fafasis, brosoch, ownsoch, sisoch, mobrosoch, fabrosoch, *fafasisch*
	tsoi	brodach, sisdach, fasisdach, mobrodach
	bizhi	*fabro*, fasis, famosisch, fafabroch, fasissosoch, *fafasisch*, mosissoch
	d'ai	mofasisso, mofabroso, momosisso, momobroso, mobro
	k'ai	mofasisda, mofabroda, momosisda, *mosis*, mobroda
	zeedi	mobroda, fasisda
	maa'aash	mobroso, fasisso
	Naai	Elbro
	Tsili	yobro
	deezhi	yosis
	adi	Elsis

* For uninitiated readers, mo=mother, sis=sister, da=daughter, ch=child, el=elder, yo=younger, and so on.
† An italicized kin description indicates that alternate terms are applied.
‡ The term -*nali* is commonly extended in politeness to nonrelatives.

5

Residence, Mobility, and Land Tenure

S OME ETHNOLOGISTS have described the Navajo as nomads, while others have
stated most definitely that they are not. The disagreement appears to arise
from conflicting definitions of the term and from the sympathies of the
ethnologists. One of the most common justifications of usurping Indian lands
has been the argument that they were nomads and thus did not put the vast
territories they used to proper use. Anthropologists and other friends of the Navajo
thus were often pressured by their own sympathy for the people to deny the
charges of the land-grabbers. In fact the Navajo do not and, it would appear,
never have wandered aimlessly behind their herds in search of grass and water.
Probably no such people has ever existed. Nonetheless, all authorities agree that
the living patterns of the Navajo are, for the most part, extremely mobile. The
life of the people in Nez Ch'ii supports such a description. In some parts of the
reservation, natural or artificial conditions have made it possible to develop what
can be best described as oases where regular crops of corn, melons, pumpkins,
grapes, peaches, and grains such as oats, wheat, and barley can be produced and
where the farmer can establish a permanent abode. However, over much of the
reservation, a Navajo homestead group must be prepared to shift its location
fairly regularly. For some, the shift comes twice a year as the herds are moved
from the lowlands to the cooler highlands in the summer and, in some cases,
from the snowy uplands to more temperate valleys in the winter. Such people generally fall into the classification of transhumants. In the Nez Ch'ii country such
clearly defined movement does not occur, although during the summer a number
of temporary sheep camps spring up as people from hotter and more arid regions
drift into the area. For the permanent residents the pattern is more complex and
entails consideration of grazing, water, wood supply, ritual beliefs, and the dynamics of the homestead group itself.

Traditional Use Area

For the most part, people in the Nez Ch'ii area answer a direct question about their mobility by saying they seldom or never move. However, more detailed questioning—asking an informant to point out on a map where he has lived during his lifetime—reveals a pattern of regular and frequent movement of the homestead group. One such informant, a boy of seventeen, could point out eleven separate locations where the homestead group had established itself in his lifetime. In addition, he recounted an annual move into winter quarters in the fall of each year and the establishment of separate mobile sheep camps during many summer periods. His experience is very much the same as those of his neighbors. The contrast between the claim that they do not move and the actual instance of movement appears to stem from the Navajo view about land tenure. Unlike many nomadic people in the Old World or the Plains Indians, the Navajo unit of movement is the homestead group or the nuclear family. Thus, no large-scale tribal or band migrations take place. Because the unit of movement is smaller, so is the size of the sheep herd. Thus, migrations in the Old World often are hundreds of miles long because the animals of the entire tribe are treated as a unit, and grazing lands must be sought for all of them. The Navajo, on the other hand, considers only the need of his own sheep herd and thus moves within a much more restricted area. Each herd, unless drought or another serious emergency forces other arrangements, moves within what has come to be called a *traditional use area*, that is, the land on which the family and its ancestors have regularly grazed their animals. Depending on the range, the water supply, and the weather, this use area may be quite small, and its efficient use may never require the moving of the base camp of the homestead group. In other instances, two areas, often widely separated, are identified with a single group that uses them alternately at different times of the year. Over most of the reservation, each homestead group will have a single contiguous use area. The condition of the range and the water supply in such an area means that an average herd must graze over an extremely large range in the course of the year, and, for convenience, the homestead must often be shifted. The most important factor in determining whether the land will support permanent occupation is the water supply. Inasmuch as the sheep herd is penned each night at the homestead, there must be adequate water sources near enough to permit the round trip to water and back. If these are limited in number, the repeated use of the same route will soon exhaust the grazing and force the homestead group to move so that the spring or well may be approached from a different direction. If a water source is so far away that the drive cannot be made and still allow time for grazing, the camp must be temporarily or permanently moved. In times past, it was often necessary for people from the Nez Ch'ii area to drive their animals in the summer to the Tuba City region, where a shallow canyon contains a river that provided permanent water for the herds. This annual migration was nearly eighty miles one way. Since the beginning of this century, the government has put down many wind-driven wells and assisted in the improvement of natural water sources, which have made such long trips unnecessary. However, until very recently, in some areas water was so limited that sheep were watered only every second or third day. Even a homestead which has several alternative water sources for its livestock is forced to move periodically, as the grass in all directions from the homesite eventually is eaten away.

As reservation lands have gradually filled with people, the traditional use areas claimed by each homestead group have grown smaller. In general, this has been a result of divisions of the original range utilized by a founding ancestor by his or her descendents. However, many homestead groups operate in an area of as much as fifteen thousand acres or more. The boundaries of such areas are recognized by the entire community, although it is often difficult for an investigator to draw a map from descriptions given by residents in the area unless the boundary is actually visited and the important landmarks demarking one grazing area from the other are pointed out. Often the boundary lines are disputed by neighbors, so that each area is surrounded by a vague zone of conflicting claims. In the past, such conflicts were resolved by shifting to new range. Today they constitute a matter of increasing social tension. Neither legally nor traditionally can these areas be considered private property. Only the right to graze sheep is effectively controlled by the homestead group. Free-ranging cattle and horses graze without reference to even these vague boundaries. Neighbors always have a claim on water sources if their own range does not have any. Trails cut directly cross country, often passing within a few feet of a hogan without reference to "ownership."

Factors of Mobility

WATER SUPPLY

If the water generally used by an outfit disappears during a drought, permission to water one's herd at a spring or well on the range of another grazer must be sought. Usually such arrangements can be made between related homestead groups. If the distance is too great to make the round trip in a single day, a temporary sheep camp will be established on the neighboring range, although the herd will be grazed on the home range as much as possible. In the past two decades a system of grazing permits issued by the tribe and government has attempted to limit overgrazing, and a committee of local grazers in each area has served to manage the range and communal operations such as branding, vaccination, and dipping. The committee often makes its decisions by articulating traditional range usages with the rules and regulations imposed from above.

Water for human use has become a less and less important factor in determining the location of a homestead since the introduction of wagons (later trucks) and barrels. Today and for several decades past, drinking water has been hauled from reliable water sources as much as thirty or forty miles away.

CROP LOCATION

The location of cornfields seldom influences the site of the homestead. If possible, it is desirable to live near one's fields, but because some areas are more suitable for crops than others and the demands of the herd are more immediate, fields may in fact be several miles from the homestead. At harvest time a temporary camp may be set up near the field to protect the crops.

FUEL SUPPLY

Fuel is a constant problem, but seldom does nearness of a wood supply influence the establishment of a homestead, save perhaps in the winter. One can use a wagon to haul large supplies of wood to the homesite rather than depend on daily foraging expeditions. In the winter, however, some consideration is given to nearby sources of fuel because it may be impossible, even with a wagon, to bring large fuel supplies through the snow drifts. Moreover, trees provide a modicum of protection from the often bitter weather.

SEASONS

The main site of a homestead is that generally occupied from early spring until the beginning of the cold season. This is seldom in the flat bottoms of the valleys, where sudden summer cloudbursts often create furious floods. Rather, the homesteads are located on the alluvial fan that spreads out around the base of the hills and mesas. The growth of juniper or piñon pine, which generally clusters

The winter camps are set up on the tops or flanks of the mesas to be near a fuel supply and to get some protection from the weather.

A typical hogan standing on the plain abandoned for the winter, while its occupants live in a more sheltered winter camp.

at the foot of the mesa itself, is often avoided because it spawns large numbers of viciously annoying flies in the hot months and is also more apt to be the habitat of snakes. Most generally, then, the summer homestead is located on the barren slopes; the surrounding grass and sage have been grazed to nothing, unprotected by trees. Shade is provided by building brush ramadas near the cabins or hogans. The various hogans and cabins may be set close together surrounding the sheep pen, itself a structure of untrimmed juniper and pine logs. More often, the homestead group will be dispersed with only one or two hogans together in one place, while other members of the group live up to a mile away.

When the winter sets in, the outfit draws closer together because the demands of the herd are much greater and require the cooperation of as many people as possible. Not infrequently, all the adults and older children must spend much of a winter day trudging on the range and stamping snow away from the scanty graze to provide feed for the herd. Winter hogans cluster close together and are usually smaller than the house at the main camp.

Temporary camps established in the summer are often nothing more than walls of brush set up against some natural object such as a standing rock or large bush. Perhaps a few blankets or pieces of canvas will be used to make the roof less porous.

The Changing Pattern of Mobility

The actual ownership of grazing lands on the Navajo reservation rests in the legal entity of the Navajo tribe and is held in trust for the tribe by the U.S. Government in order to prevent the tragic loss of land that accompanied the shifting of land to individual and tribal control among many Indian groups in the last century. Individual Navajo often strive to improve their grazing lands principally through making improvements on natural water sources. At the same time, the tribe and the Bureau of Indian Affairs attempt to maintain controls over range and water development, livestock grazing, and other matters. Income from leasing the rights to drill for oil or extract other minerals with which the reservation is richly endowed accrues to the tribe rather than to individuals. While individual families may move freely on and off the reservation and settle anywhere they wish, they must, if they wish to move their sheep herd, obtain permission from the tribal institutions involved in range management as well as secure concurrence of their new neighbors.

In the past, the long treks in search of water and grazing made the Navajo a clearly nomadic people, but the restrictions brought about by increased population, government and tribal regulations, and the increased availability of water have changed the patterns of their lives considerably. Nonetheless, they remain highly mobile people. In any year the individual will most likely live in two camps—summer and winter—and possibly more if the conditions call for the setting up of camps near the fields or a separate sheep camp. Always reacting to the demands of the sheep herd, which dominates his life as it did that of his grandfather, he will shift homesites many times during his lifetime within the scope of the traditional use area of his family. Finally, the death of a member of the family means the abandoning of his hogan and the entire homesite until the hogan has disintegrated. Other hogans in the homestead will often be dis-

One form of hogan made with upright wall logs.

assembled and transported to a new site. In recent years, because the Navajo have increasingly taken gravely ill persons to modern hospitals, their deaths in a hospital preclude the need to move.

The Adaptability of the Hogan

The core of the Navajo homestead is the distinctive hogan. Even families that prefer to live in a cabin or modern house usually build a hogan in which to have ceremonies. Many nuclear units have two hogans, one for storage. The hogan appears in a number of variations. Less frequently seen today is the oldest form, which consists of a number of logs set into the ground to form a point with a small alcove or gallery entrance constructed on one side. The wooden structure is then covered with earth. More common is one or another variation of a style called the "six-sided" or "eight-sided" hogan made of either horizontal logs chinked with mud and roofed over with earth and logs or shorter logs set into the ground in a rough circle and roofed in the same manner. Often the entire structure is covered with earth to form a dark room that is cool in the summer and warm in the winter, when a blanket or wooden hatch is used to keep rain or snow from entering the smoke hole.

6

The Animals

NAVAJO SOCIETY and culture was profoundly affected when the partially agricultural hunters and gatherers who were the ancestors of the modern Navajo chose to adopt livestock introduced by the Spanish. The older residents of the region, the Puebloan peoples, were too closely wedded to their agricultural past to exploit the potential of animal husbandry completely, although they did begin to maintain herds as an adjunct to farming. The other Apache groups, for various reasons, remained primarily raiders, seizing horses to ride in war and hunting and taking other livestock to eat. The Navajo, no less addicted to raiding for livestock, chose to maintain herds and place primary reliance on them. The general outlines of Navajo culture and many of its details then became those of nomadic or seminomadic pastoralists. Livestock—particularly horses, sheep, and goats—became the prime measure of wealth. Large herds were the goal of all Navajo, and the welfare of the herds became the central focus of Navajo life.

For the pastoralist, life must be oriented around the needs and habits of his animals. Daily and annual routines, attitudes, motor habits, and even social institutions must be planned in such a way that the demands of the herds are never left unmet. The following sections will describe Navajo society and culture from the point of view of the herds and the ways in which their owners live in order that they may be maintained.

Pastoralism gives a society greater potential for rapid territorial and population expansion than does agriculture. While the farmer must exploit enough land to feed his population, he on the other hand can seldom exploit much more than that because the amount of land to be worked is dependent upon the people available to farm it. The herder can handle two hundred animals with as much ease as one hundred, so that it is possible to expand wealth greatly without a corresponding expansion of population. However, his expanded herds demand grazing land and thus the pressure to extend territory is inherent in any pastoral society.

Before their defeat in the 1860s, Navajo culture combined raiding and herding, the former to increase the number of livestock and to obtain from

Europeans material goods that the Navajo could not produce himself. But a third element, trade, was becoming increasingly important even in these warlike times. Navajo trading parties loaded with heavy woolen Navajo rugs annually traveled to Fort Bridger in Wyoming. Wool, rugs, horses, and other livestock were readily traded for manufactured goods, often with the very people who had been raided only a short time before.

After the defeat, incarceration, and establishment of the reservation, the Navajo, in the main, abandoned warfare and raiding, at least against the dominant Anglo–American culture. Living in a land that held little attraction for American settlers but which was eminently suitable to the needs of the herdsman, the Navajo people developed a modified culture that for six decades provided a basis for expansion of population and territory and, overall, a generally satisfactory level of existence. Today, Navajo population has far outstripped the ability of the land to support it by herding. However, in Nez Ch'ii herding is still a primary activity, and the needs of livestock dominate patterns of thought and action. Nez Ch'ii today, as it was in the past, remains as the consequence of the complex interaction of men, animals, and land. The link between man and the land is the animals he keeps. It is useful, then, to look at the animals of Nez Ch'ii as a first step in understanding the Navajo who live in this region.

In general, animals can be divided into three types, based not on species but on the use to which they are put by man (*cf.* Downs, 1964, for a more detailed discussion).

Utilitarian Animals

THE HORSE

No Navajo in the Nez Ch'ii area feels comfortable unless he can speak of himself as the owner of a horse, but the discomfort is not entirely a matter of social status; a family without access to riding and draft stock is severely handicapped in the simple business of survival. Although perhaps a third to a half of the people today have some access to pick-up trucks, I did not discover a single homestead that did not have at least one, and usually two or more, horses. The wagon and the riding horse are still important methods of transport in the area. Particularly in periods of bad weather when most roads are impassable to automotive traffic, a wagon is indispensable for hauling wood and water and traveling to and from the trading store. To say a man is so poor he "don't even own no horse" is a comment not only on his social standing but also on his capacity simply to survive. However, the extension of the reservation system of paved roads into the Nez Ch'ii area is encouraging the purchase of trucks and automobiles, and the number of these vehicles nearly doubled in the year 1960–1961. The purchase of wagons and harness at the traders has dropped off considerably, as even those families without automotive transportation are looking forward to the day when they can buy an auto or truck.

The problems of the horse-keeper are not the same as those dealt with by the herder of sheep and cattle. First of all, the horse must be available for use. The degree of availability is determined by the distance one must travel to find a grazing

One of the last wagons to be sold in the Nez Ch'ii area standing in the back of the trading post. Few Navajo buy wagons today; they prefer to buy automobiles even in remote areas, where they save money against the day better roads are built.

horse and by the condition of the animal. Horses tend to drift rather far afield when they are turned out to graze, and they quickly learn that if they are close to the homestead they will be rounded up and used more often. If a man must walk ten miles to find his team, it will be used only when absolutely necessary. Some owners hobble their horses to limit their travels, and although Navajo horses are adept at moving while hobbled, the primary advantage is that an animal so handicapped can be caught more easily when finally located. At homesteads where there are enough horses available, one animal may be kept tethered to a post near the hogan, and saddled, ready for immediate use. This makes it possible to ride in search of the rest of the horse herd that has been turned out to graze. If such a surplus horse is not available, or if there is no nearby horse that can be borrowed, the homesteader must walk, often as far as ten or fifteen miles. Once the animals are located, it is customary to seek out a nearby hogan or sheep camp and borrow a horse to use in rounding up one's stock. Such loans may be made either willingly or reluctantly, but they always seem to be made.

Most homesteads boast a horse corral, but feed must be purchased for horses kept in the corral for any length of time, so such restrictions are kept to a minimum. If it is known that some member of the family will soon require a mount or team, the horses may be brought in and kept coralled for a day or two. If no hay is available, they may be turned out to graze with a boy to watch them or, in season, fed corn husks and ears (after the humans have eaten the kernels). Keeping horses in the corral creates the additional chore of driving them to water twice daily, a job usually usurped by the oldest boy in the homestead. The privilege of riding a horse is prized, and the prerogative of the elder is jealously guarded.

One factor working against the permanent corralling of horses is the Navajo belief, quite well founded in fact, that animals allowed to graze are in better condition for hard work.

Horse husbandry cannot be considered as simply a facet of the other herding activities of a family because the habits of the horse differ greatly from those of sheep and cattle. When turned out to graze, horses seldom if ever remain near the sheep herds. In fact, they generally move in the opposite direction, so that while a man is herding his sheep to the west his horses may be moving at a high trot toward a waterhole far to the east. Cattle, particularly those belonging to owners with only a few calves, often are content to remain with the sheep herd. Purchased as calves and placed with the sheep, they have been conditioned to their company. Horses, on the other hand, either are purchased as grown animals or, if raised by their owners, remain with their dams separately from the sheep. Thus animal husbandry comes to have a dual cycle, one for horses and one for sheep. If the cattle holdings are large enough, the cycle is trebled. Horses and cattle seldom graze together and when confronted with bad weather react in opposite fashions, horses moving into the storm, cattle moving with it.

The horse extends the area of a family herding operation farther than do either sheep or cattle, but the extension is not uniform in all directions. The horses of a particular family usually roam in the same general direction each time they are turned out, requiring the owner to have an intimate knowledge of the land in certain directions. Moreover, the owner thus becomes obligated to certain families whom he must often question as to whether they have seen the wandering horses or from whom he must borrow a mount. In addition, horses are generally to be found on the customary range of some other family, and such range utilization is rarely reciprocal because the family whose range is thus imposed upon may find its horses grazing on the land of yet another family. It is not surprising, then, that resentments and conflicts growing out of the grazing of horses are the most frequent livestock disputes encountered in the Nez Ch'ii area.

In periods of extreme drought, like the early summer of 1961, lack of nearby water and graze forces many families to do without their horses for long periods. At such times the animals are allowed to drift into areas where the summer rains have been more frequent, often as far as twenty or even thirty miles away. Owners of such straying stock are aware that they are taking advantage of the grazing rights of others but view this with a certain sly satisfaction at thus making profit on the better luck of a distant neighbor. Although the people thus imposed upon may grumble, they cannot—in the face of a drought—protest too loudly.

THE DOG

The other important utilitarian species is the dog. In both the scientific and popular literature it has been common to compare the Navajo shepherd and his dog to European shepherds and their sheep dogs. During my stay in the Nez Ch'ii area, however, I did not see a single dog that would be considered a sheep dog by any European or Anglo–American sheep owner. Navajo dogs usually accompany their owners into the field with the sheep, but their contribution to the control and direction of the flock is indeed limited. At best they move in the same direction as the herder and "chase" the sheep in the right direction. At worst, they remain totally uninterested in the sheep and spend their time chasing jackrabbits, digging in prairie-dog holes, or lying in the shade of a bush. Their function, however, must not be underestimated. In recent years the wholesale destruction of prairie dogs, the principal food of coyotes, and intensive campaigns of hunting and trapping have reduced the coyote population appreciably and thus the threat to the sheep herd. However, in the recent past, coyote depredations against grazing sheep were common and serious, and the primary duty of the dogs that accompanied the herd was to discover and pursue such herd-raiders.

Navajo dog training is largely limited to conditioning the dog to remain with the sheep herd. This is sometimes accomplished by keeping puppies in a box in the sheep pen and feeding them there. On occasion they are nursed by a ewe, or a goat or a ewe is milked to feed the puppy. A dog thus reared will usually stay with the herd whenever it leaves the homestead area. However, many dogs never receive such conditioning and simply learn to follow their masters when the herd is taken out. Usually a dog that refuses to join the herd is stoned, kicked, and otherwise abused if it remains near the homestead.

The dog's utility, at least in the eyes of his master, does not end with the sheep herd. Perhaps because of a history marked by raids from all directions by enemies, both Indian and White, Navajo prize their dogs as guards, a job they carry out admirably. The approach of a strange rider or wagon, or the passing of an automobile or truck, excites the dogs of a homestead into paroxysms of barking. Strange livestock, particularly horses, are also noisily announced. Of not inconsiderable importance is the belief that the dogs can sense the presence of wolf men.

Another role of the homestead dogs is that of scavenger, a function that is particularly important because of the informal toilet arrangements of the average Navajo home. Small children in particular relieve their bowels wherever they happen to be. The evidence, however, quickly disappears because a defecating child is immediately circled by several none-too-patient canines. Adults who withdraw from camp to defecate are usually followed by dogs. Dogs also consume fresh horse and cow dung that may be dropped in the vicinity of the living area, thus keeping the homesite relatively free of filth and flies.

Traditionally the Navajo have used dogs in hunting to locate animals and to track down wounded game. I did not find any dogs kept specifically for this purpose, but dogs with a proclivity for jumping rabbits and giving chase were not discouraged. One man who enjoyed hunting wildcats in the winter spoke of getting a hunting dog to assist him in tracking.

Most dogs found about a Navajo homesite are males, some of them castrated. Female puppies are usually fondled and petted for a few weeks and eventually killed to keep the population within bounds. Females that survive usually whelp in a cave or remote ravine and keep their puppies hidden until they can fend for themselves.

They haunt homesites to steal food for their broods and hunt rabbits and rodents as well. The litters seldom escape the eyes of bands of boys who roam the hills in play, and generally the puppies are brought home as pets.

Ownership of dogs, like that of other livestock, is individual. Each dog is associated with a nuclear family and is referred to as "Alta's dog" or "Kee's dog" in reference to the man or woman in the family. However, further inquiry usually reveals that within the nuclear group dogs have various owners, with each member of the group owning a dog if the family can afford it. The number of dogs varies, as a Navajo would put it, according to "whether you likes dogs or not," but everyone obviously feels that he or she should own a dog. The establishing of claims on a new litter of puppies is one source of friction within the extended family. Whether the bitch is owned by the homestead or not, puppies are usually "found," either abandoned by owners who do not want them or hidden by their mothers. The practice of killing unwanted puppies at birth seems unknown, and puppies are usually turned out near a well-traveled road, or at the trader's, or at a spring or well, so that someone will discover them and take them home. The discovery of a new litter immediately sets off competition among a number of children over the puppies. Not infrequently, the puppies are taken away from the mother and handled until they die. If they survive, there is a regular struggle between the family and the mother, who tries to relocate her brood and carry it away, although usually she will finally simply come in to feed the puppies periodically. If the puppies survive, adults who want a dog generally override the claims of children by appropriating the animal, usually when the child making the claim is absent. There may also be competition between adults, and such disputes sometimes lead to actual fist fights between adult women. Until the animal is fairly well grown and its ownership well established, the owner, child or adult, must be prepared to defend his or her claim against other members of the extended family.

Dogs encountered on the range away from any habitation may be shot, or shot at, if a gun is handy, but if the Navajo is mounted, it is very likely that he will uncoil his lariat and attempt to rope the animal. In such encounters there is a great deal of concern about the animal's ownership, a concern that is natural in any sheep-herding area because of the dread of packs of wild dogs. Such packs are perhaps the most deadly threat to sheep herders in America, their depredations far exceeding that of natural predators such as mountain lions, wildcats, wolves, eagles, or coyotes.

Navajo dogs are not starved, but they are forever hungry, which creates both advantages and disadvantages. There is little refuse left near a Navajo hogan because of the dogs' appetites, nor does the offal and waste from slaughtering survive long. On the other hand, dogs are always alert to snatch food, literally from the hands or the cooking fires of their masters, and when such forays are successful, a whole family may well have a night without food.

Although the Navajo consider their dogs important and real members of the group and view them affectionately, they seldom pet them the way Whites do. Dogs are allowed on the peripheries of the eating ground but driven severely from hogans, houses, or summer shades. In the Navajo view a dog should be devoted but remain distant, and common Navajo practice insures the distance. Dogs are often called, patted briefly, then hit rather severely. Few Navajo can resist throwing a stone at a dog, but although they can be amazingly accurate, they seldom hit the dogs, thus belying their apparently vicious intent. There is general admiration for a "tough dog," and generally the dogs of a homesite are subservient to a single leader, which, as he grows older, must defend his position daily.

The Navajo tend to speak of their dogs in a kindly manner, and young men speak with some pride of a dog that refuses to eat or otherwise demonstrates sorrow at their absence or which refuses to be taken from their presence by another human.

A common occurrence is the killing of a dog by an adult male in the course of a dispute with members of the family. A man frustrated and angry after a fight with his wife may, particularly if the animal is a stray or does not belong to a member of his family, shoot and kill a dog. An example drawn from my field notes illustrates this:

May 10
Tom and his wife have been quarreling all day. I think the problem is that she and his mother don't get along. She also has become very insistent that they move out of his sister's extra house and build one of their (really her) own. Just before dusk the bickering rose to a shouting quarrel, and Tom burst out of the house with a gun in his hand. He looked absolutely outraged. Before I knew what was happening, he shot a dog five times, killing it instantly. He seemed to calm down after that and went over to Harriet's cabin where he remained until dark. Don't know when he came home. The dog was not one of the regular homestead pack but had been hanging around the edges of camp for a couple of days. All of the others in camp disappeared into their cabins or hogans and stayed there, afraid.

May 11
Asked Harriet's oldest daughter why Tom had shot the dog yesterday. She said, "Oh, he had been fighting with his wife. He was pretty mad. That's why he shot it." Today everything seemed back to normal. No quarreling at Tom's.

Although the owner of the dog may be both angry and sorrowful, he seldom takes any direct action about such a killing. A man angry enough to kill a dog, in the Navajo view, is not totally responsible, and moreover any angry person is considered dangerous and to be avoided.

Dogs are named according to the accidents of their acquisition, their individual peculiarities, or the whims of their owners. On the homestead where I lived, the names included Wine, describing the light brown color (three other dogs of the litter were named Whiskey, Beer, and Peyote); Bear, a reference to a burly build and a short tail; Ringo, after a western outlaw currently popular on television in the off-reservation boarding school; Johnny; and Supper—this last was said by some members of the family to refer to the puppy's appetite, but others said it reflected his size, which was "just enough to eat for supper." The people of the Nez Ch'ii region view dog eating as both humorous and somewhat disgusting, and certainly a trait of other and lesser Indians.

Dogs are considered the responsibility of their owners, insofar as there is any control at all save the occasional flinging of a stone. If, however, a dog successfully raids the human food supply, its owner shares the guilt, although he is not expected to make recompense. There is a high degree of anthropomorphizing in the attitude of Navajo toward their dogs. Dogs are described as tough, smart, and the like. The details of canine social and family structure are well known and remarks such as "that one—Johnny—he's Wine's son, so he always stick up for him in a fight" are common.

This attitude is in sharp contrast to that adopted toward a far more important animal, the horse. Some horses appear to be named, but usually their names refer to some characteristic, for example the "black horse," the "white mare" (gray horses are invariably spoken of as white), the "old horse," or they are identified by reference to the owner. Horses are also described as good or bad according to their ability to work, but no attributes of character are ascribed to them. White horsemen very frequently speak of a horse as having courage or loyalty, but such references are meaningless to the Navajo—except as they indicate the eccentricity of White men.

Dogs receive little or no medical attention, although their ailments are a matter of concern to their owners. The most common injuries are those incurred in fights. Often such wounds are extensive and serious, but lack of knowledge of first aid prevents treatment. A severely wounded dog is watched, and some attempt is made to keep other dogs from attacking a disabled member of the pack. Recovery from severe wounds is accepted as evidence of a dog's "toughness." If some aid is available, such as that offered by a visiting anthropologist, it is accepted gratefully and the treatment and recovery is apt to be a subject of repeated discussion.

The dog and the horse, kept in large part for their utility, present a distinct contrast in the demands their ownership makes and in the consequences their ownership has. The horse ranges widely and requires a wide extension of human relationships so that the owner may make use of him and at the same time support him by utilizing the natural range. This wide-ranging propensity of the horse is the basis of many interpersonal relationships, both friendly and hostile. In addition, in order to make the horse an effective part of the economic unit, a number of livestock artifacts must be obtained, which will be discussed in a later section. The horse also requires the expenditure of money for feed when there is extreme food shortage, when extended periods of hard work are required, and when travel is in areas where feed is not available. The dog, on the other hand, seldom ranges far away from its owner and thus seldom extends human relationships. Potentially, however, the dog is a threat to smooth human relations, inasmuch as it may raid the food supply of a neighbor, fight with and injure a neighbor's dog, or attack a neighbor's livestock. Also, the killing of a stray dog may lead to disputes with the owner. Very little effort is expended in maintaining dogs, although shepherds usually carry a gun in order to shoot rabbits for the dog to eat, and some of the animals killed in rabbit chases are given to the dogs.

Marketable Livestock

Animals in the category of marketable livestock include all species maintained for sale or consumption.

CHICKENS

Occasionally, homesteads have a few chickens wandering among the hogans. The birds are of indeterminate breed, scrawny, and often nearly featherless from some combination of ills. Occasionally, I was told, a bird will be killed and eaten, and eggs are sometimes eaten. The birds are not penned or otherwise housed in the summer. Occasionally a makeshift shelter referred to as a chicken house may be thrown up, or a covered dugout may be made, which helps the birds to survive the winter. The birds subsist on scraps from the preparation of human food and by pecking through horse and cow dung for undigested seeds. In this way they keep the homestead free of any garbage or offal missed by the dogs. The primary function of the birds seems to be to serve as targets for little boys practicing with a lariat, and as such they contribute to the development of human skills. In old literature on the Navajo the chicken is most commonly mentioned in connection with the Mexican equestrian contest of "chicken pulling." In this event a chicken is buried up to its neck, and riders attempt to seize the bird while galloping past it, a feat requiring a great deal of agility and skill. Informants in their fifties remember seeing this sport in their youth, but it has long since been abandoned. However, the Navajo word for rodeo is the same as the word for chicken.

SHEEP

Sheep dominate the livestock economics of Nez Ch'ii and the Navajo reservation as a whole. The social and cultural life of a family owning even four or five sheep is largely determined by this ownership. In part this is owing to cultural patterns built around sheep keeping as a way of life and supporting the patterns of sheep keeping as the "right" way to live. Also, the possession of even a few sheep requires certain activities that are only intensified if the number of sheep is increased. Sheep keeping also requires herding and tending every day, so that the activities of man are dominated by the needs of the herd. When the herd can provide man with his needs, the system remains in balance. In recent years, income from livestock cannot meet the needs of the Navajo, a situation that produces social and psychological tensions and sets the stage for major cultural changes.

Of all domestic creatures generally maintained by herding people, the sheep is perhaps the most thoroughly domesticated. It is doubtful whether domestic sheep could survive for a single winter without human assistance. Sheep are generally thought of, and rightly so, even by shepherds, as being unintelligent relative to other domestic animals.

HERDING INSTINCT The most notable characteristic of the domestic sheep is its herding instinct. The need to herd, the compulsion to follow others of its kind, makes it easy for a single man with or without the assistance of dogs to control several hundred sheep. A moving sheep herd is seldom plagued with the consistent herd-bolter or bunch-quitter found in almost any herd of cattle or horses. A sheep separated from its flock is almost invariably doomed. If the almost defenseless animal is not killed by predators, it starves to death or dies of thirst. A herdsman can hope for the survival of an isolated calf or colt but seldom a lamb.

Moreover, the behavior of a sheep herd is such that it cannot be permitted freedom to graze at will. Watching a herd graze, one is struck by the fact that it is in constant, nervous motion, each animal reacting to the movements of the others. This motion sometimes leads the herd to good grazing, but it may also bring the herd to a full stop, each animal reacting to another and no single animal breaking the spell. Most Navajo herds have a few goats mixed in with the sheep, and these curious, active, and self-reliant animals initiate almost all the action in the herd. Sheep are easily conditioned into simple habits, so that certain surroundings or conditions evoke a repeated response. This enables the shepherd to move animals to a specific place and then ignore them, since he is certain that they will respond by going to water or following a certain trail or drifting back into the sheep pen. The fact that sheep are so easily handled and only have to be directed rather than driven makes it possible for anyone—man, woman, or child older than seven or eight—to assume the duties of herder. In short, a Navajo child may begin his life as a herder of sheep before he is ten and continue as a herder into very old age, stopping only when he or she is no longer able to walk. Sheep, then, require a maximum of care but are easily controllable, so that a great variety of people can take part in this care.

LAMBING In the winter and particularly in early spring, sheep herding is far more arduous. The cold winds or snows usually keep the herd on the move to find grass and to avoid the worst of the weather. In the spring the problem is complicated by the lambing. Ewes are taken out with the herd and allowed to lamb in the field. This means that the shepherd must be alert to spot the ewes as they lie down in the sagebrush at the onset of labor. When the lamb is born, the herder, using a mirror, signals the homestead and someone comes out to take the lamb back. The direction of the sun in relation to the homestead is an important factor in herding at this time. If the homestead cannot be signaled or if several lambs have been born, the herder usually starts a fire and keeps the lambs warm until either he or someone else can take the animals home. His job is complicated by the fact that the ewes that have already lambed are also with the herd. These animals constantly attempt to leave the herd and return to the homestead where the young lambs are kept. As the season progresses and the number of lambed ewes increases, a major part of the herd may be constantly attempting to bolt for home.

HERDING METHODS Anglo–American commercial sheep operations contrast with Navajo sheep herding, in which the sheep are regularly penned. Anglo–American methods fall into two classes, range techniques and fenced techniques. In the first, large herds are cared for by shepherds with the assistance of dogs. The sheep herd is moved slowly over a wide area, the herder accompanying the herd in a trailer home or tent. Movement is dictated by the condition of the range. When feed is exhausted, the herd is shifted to another range. Consideration must be given to the availability of water, but the primary pattern is the constant shift to new range that is grazed once each season. In certain areas and at certain times of the year, sheep may be maintained on fenced range without the constant surveillance of a shepherd or his dogs. Sometimes such operations are relatively small scale— a farmer maintaining a few head of sheep just as he keeps a few pigs, a head or two of cattle, and some chickens—but in other operations rather large numbers of sheep are kept under fenced conditions during lambing or in the process of fattening for market. Purebred sheep are often raised entirely in this manner.

Navajo herding methods combine close control with the open range. Perhaps because of a history of livestock keeping marked by raiding and counter-raiding, or perhaps because of the not inconsiderable fear most Navajo have of the dark, sheep are penned each night. The only exceptions to this in my experience were when herds were being moved and could not be penned, or when a herd was being held overnight near a dipping vat so that it might be dipped early in the morning. In both these situations the animals were closely herded and carefully watched. When it is necessary to pen sheep away from the homestead, they are penned if possible in an abandoned pen or a box canyon.

In addition to the nightly penning, sheep in the Nez Ch'ii area are penned during the heat of the day. This period begins when the sun is well up, about 9 A.M. in the summer and somewhat later or not at all in the winter. Although the heat in the Nez Ch'ii area is not intense, the Navajo here appear to be culturally conditioned toward an extreme sensitivity and consider it hot when the thermometer goes past 80°F. Their sheep react to heat by refusing to graze and by standing bunched together, each animal attempting to shade its eyes by sticking its head under its neighbor. It is virtually impossible for a shepherd to make a herd move once it has stopped. The shouts and blows of the herder, even assisted by dogs, seldom do more than force a few animals to shift position. Attacks on the flock by coyotes are reported to cause little disturbance. Thus, the Navajo has a choice of remaining with the herd throughout the day or getting it home and penned before the sun gets too high. The latter course is usually followed because it does not tie up the services of the herder during the midday meal. On cool days or when the herd is grazing near the homestead, it may not be brought in and penned but simply watched by whoever is around, or the younger children may be assigned to keep an eye on the animals. If, however, the herd is out of sight when caught by the sun, it is a matter of great concern, and the entire homestead begins searching until the animals and the herder are located.

The herd is generally taken out to graze just before dawn and kept on the range until the sun begins to get high, about 9 A.M. The animals are then penned through the heat of the midmorning and early afternoon and turned out for grazing again about 4 P.M. They are penned for the night shortly before sunset. On the long summer day, the herd is permitted to graze about seven and one-half hours out of the twenty-four. This patterning of grazing is, of course, determined by circumstances; for example, the pattern described above is the one followed on a homestead with a large water supply only a few hundred yards from the homesite. With slight modifications, it is the one followed by any herd that can be driven to water and back to the pen within the time limits. In some cases the herd must be held on the range during the still period in order to reach distant water that may be as far as from five to ten miles away from the homestead. Where the herd must go as far as ten miles for water, there is a strong tendency to shift camp because twenty miles in the course of a day is an extremely long drive for a sheep herd. A round trip of ten miles, however, is not at all unusual.

The shifting of the herd from the homestead to a sheep camp is not casually undertaken. Such a shift usually means that the herd must trespass on the grazing land of other families, and negotiation for permission must be undertaken. Usually this is done by a relative of the moving family who has married into the host family. For instance, if a brother is living with his wife on land that would be trespassed, he is asked to go to his father-in-law or mother-in-law to obtain permission for his family to camp near the water source. In addition, informal permission must be obtained from the grazing committee representative for the move. Once permission is obtained, one of the nuclear families is chosen to go to the camp. Invariably such groups isolated from the rest of the outfit express "fear" and report the appearance of wolf men, strange sounds, or very real intrusions of "drunkers." At the same time, the families remaining at the homestead often say they are "lonesome." Frequent trips between the homestead and the sheep camps are made on almost any pretext. Usually the first family is followed by yet another and as often as not the entire homestead will have shifted, in the course of a few days or a week or two, from the outfit to the camp. In addition, if a member of the outfit lives with his wife's family near the new location, he visits his relatives more often and perhaps brings his wife and family to live in the camp temporarily. At the same time, if intraoutfit frictions have developed, which frequently do during such periods of water shortage, the sheep camp provides a mechanism for increasing distance between quarreling members. Usually at least one family remains at the homestead to watch the property. With two such bases of operation, individual members can move back and forth to avoid conflict within the group.

My own observations and conversations with informants lead me to believe that the pattern of penning during the day is, and always has been, the preferred method of keeping sheep, but that in former times before the drilling of wells and creation of catchment dams, it was more often necessary to keep the herd out all day on the trip to water. Today, in times of drought when the windmill wells go dry and the dam water is exhausted, the long drive must be undertaken. In the winter when the days are shorter and the temperature is low, the herds are frequently kept out all day.

Today, under extreme drought conditions, the use of trucks to haul water makes it possible for at least some homesteads to weather the dry period without shifting camp. Informants estimated that a herd of two hundred and fifty sheep require about one thousand gallons of water daily. Their estimate was based on the number of fifty-five-gallon drums they hauled during the most recent dry spell. Under these conditions the entire effort of the homestead is required to graze and water the herd; two men were employed all day in hauling water, and the rest of the family was needed to water the sheep, which were released from the pen ten head at a time. It might be mentioned here that any operation that requires single sheep or small groups of sheep to be separated (for counting, drinking, vaccination, and so on) is extremely difficult. Such an operation calls for as many hands as can be mustered, so strong is the predilection of one sheep to follow another.

In the deep winter when the snow covers the grass, it is necessary for the entire homestead to devote its energy to uncovering feed for the herd. This means that all adults and older children spend the whole day with the herd and stamp the snow away from the grass.

This grazing and penning pattern quickly exhausts the range in two areas, the one immediately around the homestead where the herd grazes upon entering and leaving the living area and the one around water sources, dams, springs, or wells. Each of these areas is picked barren, with the greatest damage being done, of course, in the vicinity of water, for while the homestead can be and often is shifted, the water source cannot. However, some homesteads may not move because of the construction of permanent water facilities, or a desire to be near certain neighbors or the trading post. Around such homesteads the land is stripped bare, and even the sagebrush is reduced to stumps. In other areas of the reservation where the summer temperatures are higher and water scarcer, it is still common to move the herd into summer ranges and for at least part of the homestead group to live at a temporary sheep camp. In the Nez Ch'ii area few people are forced to do this because of relatively low temperatures, a fairly constant supply of grass, and a number of alternative water sources. However, a few families move into the peripheries of the Nez Ch'ii region from less-favored areas. Among the permanent residents there is a friendly contempt for these "sheep camps" but apparently no open hostility. To the east, around Nazlini Wash, almost the entire population vacates the area in the summer to move into sheep camps in the Lukachukai Mountains.

BREEDING   Generally speaking, sheep will breed at any time of the year. In practice, however, sheepherders attempt to prevent breeding before mid-October to insure the birth of lambs in the late spring. This gives the young the advantage of maturing during favorable weather. Early-born lambs are subject to the bad weather that may occur in early spring, and lambs born too late in the spring are not mature enough to survive the winter. The practice of keeping rams away from ewes until October is relatively new among the Navajo and is still not universally practiced. To separate the rams requires two herding and penning operations or the permanent penning of the males with the requirement that food must be purchased or collected to maintain them. One alternative method is to install an apron around the loins of rams that does not hinder elimination but covers the genitals of the ewe should she be mounted. In this way the rams can be herded with the rest of the herd, although, as with most methods of contraception, failures are frequent. Another alternative is for Navajo herders to use the rams supplied by the tribe from its experimental Ban N ranch and brought into the area at the proper time for breeding.

Government extension agents have advocated the late breeding of sheep to avoid the bad weather of early spring since they contend that lambs dropped later have a better chance for survival. Generally speaking, this is supported by the experience of sheepherders throughout the United States. However, the Navajo practice of early breeding and lambing may in fact not be as detrimental as the experts suggest. The structure of the Navajo extended family makes it possible for a great many man-hours to be devoted to caring for lambs. A regular night watch is maintained by each outfit; keeping a fire burning, members of the watch stay up all night in order to prevent the lambs from freezing and to care for any lambs dropped in the night. During the day, lambs are kept in the sheep pen and protected from the weather. If the weather turns bad, lambs are placed in small dugouts roofed over with branches and earth. Lambs that do poorly are fed with milk, either canned or surplus powdered milk. Canned milk of the Carnation or Pet brands is much preferred, the Navajo claiming that lambs do not like other canned brands or powdered milk. Although this kind of care requires a high investment of human effort under far from pleasant conditions, it results in a surprisingly high ratio of surviving lambs. Moreover, early lambing permits nursing ewes to take full advantage of the early spring grasses and the plentiful water supply of the season, and lambs beginning to graze enjoy the advantage of a large quantity of good spring grass. One of the major livestock problems on the reservation is the failure of many lambs to reach marketable weight (thirty-five to forty-five pounds minimum) in time for fall marketing. The tribe regularly purchases these unmarketable "peewee" lambs and later sells them at a loss in an emergency buying program. However, in the Nez Ch'ii area, where early lambing is still common, very few lambs fail to reach marketable weight, and the emergency purchases are limited to mature goats and barren ewes. This suggests that the traditional methods based on the structure of the Navajo family are better suited to the reservation environment than the "modern" methods advocated by the government.

The stock-reduction and the stock-improvement program have resulted in a general improvement of Navajo sheep, which were in the recent past notably unimproved and considerably less than efficient in meat and wool production. Indications of this unimproved blood are still to be seen in Navajo herds, particularly in remote areas. Most noticeable are the multiple-horned rams, having three, four, and occasionally five horns sprouting from their foreheads. Another sign of scrub blood is mixed-color wool. Many Navajo sheep are to be seen bearing wool of every shade from white to black, with many shades of grey, brown, and red. Such wool requires considerably more work to separate and is therefore less valuable in the market. Nevertheless, when hand-carded and spun, this wool is useful in the production of natural-colored Navajo rugs, which are sometimes made entirely without dye.

MARKETING   Spring, in addition to being the season for lambing, is also the time for sheepshearing and the sale of wool. Every effort is made to be on hand to assist during lambing at this time of year, and shearing requires the efforts of all members of the homestead group, except of course the children who are away at school or those members who must be absent in the course of work. At this time the wool is marketed, most of it going directly to the Indian trader for cash or credit.

The late spring and summer is a period during which the sheep herd is counted, dipped, and vaccinated, and, as the summer progresses, any animals to be marketed are selected. There is no clear-cut market period. Late in the summer the trader announces he is purchasing sheep and cattle, and the animals are brought in individually or in small bunches by their owners. Several such sales may be made during the fall by a single owner as he needs money. When the trader has collected a number of sheep, a commission agent hauls the animals away to feed lots to be fattened prior to marketing. However, the trader will usually purchase sheep at any time during the year, although his prices may be so low as to discourage very many offerings. In addition, the trader maintains on feed perhaps a dozen head of sheep (often old and barren ewes, sold because they are not productive), and from time to time he slaughters one of these animals for sale at his own butcher counter.

Navajo father sharpening his shears before beginning to shear a sheep in the early spring.

GOATS

Goats are in most respects the social and cultural equivalent of sheep. They are herded with the sheep, dipped, vaccinated, and sheared at the same time and, except at counting times, considered simply as part of the sheep herd. However, there are notable and important differences between goats and sheep. Despite the similarity of the animals, the goat is far more independent of man and, as has often been proved, quite able to survive without man's protection. The goat is curious, active, and far more adventurous than the sheep. Goats are usually satisfied with rougher food and are able to subsist on all sorts of brush that sheep prefer not to eat except when driven by hunger. The goats in a sheep herd, and there are always a few, act as both the sentinels and leaders of the herd, and the sudden dashes from food source to food source that often mark the progress of the herd are invariably led by goats. Goats add to the burden of pen building because they are more determined in their efforts to escape and because they climb and jump with amazing agility. Some pens are constructed with a stile that permits the goats to leave and enter at will but keeps the sheep contained. This device in a way symbolizes a vaguely expressed difference in attitude toward the two species on the part of the Navajo. The herd, for instance, is always spoken of as the "sheep herd," or "the sheep," although in fact most of the animals may be goats. This attitude is difficult to describe exactly—the Navajo simply appear to be less interested in goats. It may stem from the fact that sheep are viewed as the food animal par excellence, and mutton is surrounded with all the connotations of home, comfort, and good living. Mutton hunger is a recognized condition of Navajo who must live away from the family herds. "I want some fresh mutton," means that the speaker in fact does want some mutton to eat, but it also carries the connotation of homesickness and, I suspect, an allusion to young, unsophisticated back-country girls. Goats are eaten, but much less often than sheep. At Squaw-Dance feasts the ratio of goats to sheep is perhaps one to four. Goats are occasionally milked, and possibly in the past cheese was made, but I found no evidence of cheese making at the time of my visit. Until perhaps three decades ago most goats were of nondescript milking breeds, and goat milk was an important part of the Navajo diet. The shift to angora goats in an attempt, not particularly successful, to raise cash income has adversely affected nutrition, especially that of children.

Goats supply mohair and are most often of the angora or long-haired type in colors ranging from white through pale tans and browns to mixed colors and pure black. Mohair is currently selling for a higher price than wool. However, most Navajo do not seem inclined to increase the number of goats in their herds at the expense of their sheep holdings. The most common reason is that the long goat hair makes it extremely hard for the animals to winter in the snow-bound uplands. The tightly curled greasy wool of sheep tends to insulate them from the cold, but goat hair gathers mud and snow in frozen balls, threatening the animals with immobilization and freezing. (It might be pointed out that the cropping of sheep's tails is done to prevent the balling of mud and snow, which will literally anchor an undocked sheep in bad weather.) The final special problem in goat husbandry, although minor, is extremely annoying to the owner. The brush and leafy tree-limb roofing of the summer shade under which a great part of the life of the Navajo is carried out is unfailingly attractive to goats, which strip the shade and the shade roof if not watched. The sight of a goat peacefully browsing on the roof while his owners try to dislodge him with thrown sticks and stones is a common summer scene.

CATTLE

Cattle are the only other animals kept for economic or marketing purposes. Without exception, the animals are beef cattle, and with only a few exceptions they are the common "whiteface" of the Western cattle industry. A "whiteface" is in fact a grade animal descended from the introduction of Hereford and shorthorn blood into the herds of Texas or Mexican cattle common in the West until the 1880s and 1890s. There have been infusions of most other beef brands into this range pool, but the Hereford characteristics of red body contrasted with white belly and face mark the majority of Western range cattle, including those of the Nez Ch'ii area.

It is a rule of thumb that it requires a breeding herd of 150 cows to maintain an adequate income in the United States. In 1957, there were 665 mature cattle grazing in the Nez Ch'ii area. Of these, "over a hundred" were reportedly owned by a single owner near Hard Rocks and "almost a hundred" by another wealthy man (by Navajo standards) who lives near the trading post. Other herds are appreciably smaller, with twenty to thirty head being considered a "lot of cattles" by the Navajo of the area. Many cattle owners boast only one, two, or three head. Most of these animals are breeding stock, that is, cows that produce calves for market and / or female calves to be kept to enlarge the breeding herds. As mentioned earlier, if an owner possesses more than a single cow, his livestock operation takes on another dimension in addition to the horse and sheep complex described above. Cattle are often obtained as weaned calves, perhaps six or eight months old. Not infrequently, such animals are what is colloquially called "dougy" (dogy) calves, that is, they do not have mothers, or the mother cannot feed them. Such animals may simply be turned out with the sheep herd of a small owner and become quickly conditioned to the environment; they seldom wander far from the sheep and goats and become part of the herd for all practical purposes. However, if the number of cattle increases beyond one or at the most two, the picture changes, and the two or three head form a cattle herd inasmuch as they require special allocation of time and effort on the part of the herdsman.

GRAZING PATTERN It is part of the folklore of the West that cattle and sheep will not occupy the same range or use the same waterholes and that the entry of sheep into a cattle range drives the cattle off. This generalization, of course, is untrue as an unqualified statement, but there are differences in the range utilization by the two species. In part because cattle are kept under less restraint and in part because they require four times the range per head, they range far more widely than do sheep and goats, although not so far as horses. Sheep can and do graze ground-cover much more closely than do cattle and are able to consume many plants not normally considered palatable for cattle. This means that a sheep herd can remain for a longer period on the same ground and still benefit. Cattle, having grazed an area as closely as they can, move on, so even if sheep and cattle were herded together, they would gradually separate as the cattle ranged farther and farther afield while the sheep remained on the original ground. Observations made of a single herd suggest that five miles from the homestead is generally the normal limit of cattle wandering. The wandering of cattle, like that of horses, is not random but tends to extend itself in specific directions according to the distribution of food plants and the availability of water. Only the herd conditioning of a single calf raised with sheep would keep it relatively close to the sheep herd. If the calf had the company of another of its kind, the cattle would soon separate from the sheep and drift off on their own. To prevent this would require that the sheep herd constantly move or that the herder continually drive the cattle back to the sheep herd. What happens in fact is that cattle are treated differently and considered apart from sheep. Although two or three cows or calves may be penned at night with the sheep and moved away from the homestead at the same time and in the same direction as the sheep, the herder does not keep as close a watch on them; he seldom expects them to come back to the pen at midday and in fact is not too concerned should they fail to return for a day or two. A constantly operating livestock-locating network is likely to keep him informed of the whereabouts of both his cattle and horses for many days without his actually seeing them. For example, a rider passing through the homestead or a friend met at the trader's mentions that he saw the owner's stock at a certain place as he was traveling. If the reports suggest that the animals are straying too far, or if no reports come in for several days, the owner or a relative may conduct a desultory search, usually on horseback.

If such a preliminary search does not discover the cattle somewhere on or near the owner's grazing land, he expresses real concern and sets out to search in earnest. A larger herd will probably receive more constant surveillance but generally will be expected to find water for itself, except during periods of drought when the animals must be driven to different watering places.

BULLS   The few bulls owned in the Nez Ch'ii area constitute a special problem because they are viewed as particularly dangerous (a contention not without foundation but greatly exaggerated by the Navajo), and a wandering bull is apt to create serious friction between outfits. The appearance of a bull, threatening or not, disrupts the life of an outfit, as invariably the women and children retreat to the shelter of a hogan while some of the braver men attempt to drive the animal away. In the summer of 1961 a bull belonging to a tribal policeman became a local cause celebre, as the animal became a focus for resentment toward its owner. The

The owner, in light shirt and hat, standing, supervises the branding of one of his calves at the community branding.

animals depredations were daily reported to the policeman or his family, together with threats to kill the bull. More often than not, the bull was reported in several places at one time. It was considered an excellent joke to suggest that this bull be offered to a man who was being asked to become host of a Squaw Dance, as it was rumored he did not want to accept the "honor" in return for the traditional present of four sheep, but preferred a cow instead. Finally, the policeman in desperation kept the bull in a pen and fed him hay. The situation was all the more ludicrous when one observed the children of the policeman's family playing with the bull, which had become little more than a pet and which "raided" the neighbors only out of a desire for human company.

THE ROUNDUP The most important time in the cattle owner's year is in late summer, after the community sheep dipping, when a series of community roundups are staged. The tribe supplies no working crew for the roundup, and the work is carried out by owners, members of the grazing committee, and men who are interested in cattle or, more properly, in being cowboys. It is notable that the festive air of a sheep dip is completely absent at a cattle roundup, and, in contrast to the former occasion, there are almost no women present.

At the roundup, bull calves and colts are castrated by a man who travels with the grazing committee chairman, who supervises the roundup. The most important job is that of branding the unbranded stock. Each owner has a registered brand consisting of a number indicating the grazing district and a number indicating his own herd. In addition, a Bar N is branded on the shoulder of all Navajo cattle and horses.

The roundup takes place during or shortly before the livestock-buying period at the trader's. Because most herds are extremely small and many owners

An elder looks on while younger men castrate a horse.

keep cattle only to increase their holdings, animals are usually bought one at a time; barren cows, bull calves, and steers make up the bulk of the salable animals, as they do anywhere. One or two large owners sell a number of cattle directly to commission agents. The purchased animals are held in the trader's corrals until a sufficient number have been gathered for shipping.

Occasionally, in response to the urging of his White clerks and the rest of the beef-hungry non-Indian population, the trader will butcher a beef for sale, but most of the animals are shipped out to feeders. Once branded, counted, and registered by the tribal brand inspector, the cattle are driven back to their home range. Any sale, either between Indians or off the reservation, must be registered by the brand inspector of the tribe.

SPECIAL PROBLEMS   As stated before, most herds are small and not considered as income property at present but are being kept to breed and increase by hopeful owners. To increase the size of a herd is very difficult because of grazing restrictions. Even the purchase of an animal from outside the district, although within the reservation, creates a good deal of friction and resentment. Thus, an owner builds his herd as someone else reduces his, and the overall number of animals in the district increases slowly.

Although cattle, unlike sheep, do not require the day-to-day care that is more and more resented by younger men, they present some special problems. During the winter, cattle are less able to subsist on the surviving forage than are sheep and goats, and cattle owners must often find means of obtaining some additional winter feed. One of the more common sources, if funds are available, is hay from other Navajo who live in areas where field agriculture is practiced, particularly where irrigation projects have made alfalfa production possible. In the past, during periods of heavy snow the tops of trees were cut to supply browse for both sheep and cattle, and, at least sometimes, cattle were driven into lower areas where snow was less of a problem.

There would appear to be more resentment of a large cattle herd than of a large sheep herd, perhaps because cattle are almost never slaughtered for food and thus represent a "rich man's" economic activity. It is whispered that the area's single rich man, who owns a large number of cattle, is able to maintain his large herd by "stealing" water from other people, that is, by driving his stock to springs, dams, and wells that are traditionally used and maintained by others. He is said to do this at night when other people aren't about. It is interesting, however, to compare the resentment directed toward this man, who is noted for his miserliness and who has only one child, with the attitude toward a man at Hard Rocks who is said to have even more cattle. The latter owner seems to be the target of no resentment, at least among his more distant neighbors, because "he has lots of kids."

STEALING   One other aspect of the cattle complex should be mentioned— cattle stealing. There appears to be relatively little stealing of animals by members of the district from other members of the district; the discovery of such larceny would be almost inevitable. However, there are some families living along the boundary between Navajo and the Hopi reservation who are said to make their living by stealing Hopi cattle. The informant offered this intelligence tentatively and carefully waited to judge my reaction before elaborating. Further questioning made it clear that neither he nor his neighbors felt such activities were particularly reprehensible as long as they were carried out by Navajo against Hopis, which reflects the long history of Navajo raiding against the mesa-top villagers.

The single case of cattle stealing that I was able to establish occurred in the summer of 1961 when the adopted son of the local rich man, with the help of two friends, butchered one of his father's cattle. This was considered an out-and-out theft by the Navajo, who excused it to a degree because the thieves were drunk. It was also considered excusable because the victim was rich. The thieves were three well-known ne'er-do-wells of the area, whose only occupation in the summer was to move from one Squaw Dance to another, taking advantage of the plentiful food supply at such affairs and contributing little besides their presence and singing ability. The local Navajo and the police looked briefly for the culprits but soon gave up the search. About three weeks after the incident all three men were once again seen in the area. It is possible that they had agreed to recompense the owner for his loss, an act that in the Navajo view would have closed the case. On another occasion, a woman demanded and received ten sheep from a young man who, while drunk, had stolen a blanket and some jewelry in order to buy liquor. In addition, my informants reported that because of the drought many people were suffering hardship and occasionally killed a cow from the rich man's herd. This was considered as theft but not a serious crime because the animal was killed for food and the victim was rich.

Thus we see in the livestock complex of the Nez Ch'ii region three distinct subcomplexes of land use, each requiring different techniques and bringing into play different sets of human relationships.

The Tools and Techniques of Livestock Operations

Domestication involves much more than the presence of an animal under the control of human beings. A domesticating society must have at its disposal a complex of tools, techniques, attitudes, and knowledge. Each species of animal brought under control increases the number of tools and techniques needed and expands the knowledge required. A good shepherd is not necessarily a good cowboy. Neither the shepherd nor the cowboy, by virtue of his competence in these fields, is automatically a good horse wrangler. Among the Navajo, who have adopted all three of these grazing animals into a single socioeconomic and cultural complex, it has been necessary to develop or borrow techniques to carry out the livestock operation. It might be pointed out here that in the European tradition there is at least a strong tendency for specialization in livestock operations. Although it is common for a single economic unit, such as a large ranch, to have sheep-, cattle-, and horse-raising operations contributing to its income, they tend to be definitely separated. Different sets of specialists work with different animals, and different parts of the range are used for each operation.

The Navajo have combined these three complexes rather closely. This combination is due in part to the generally small units of livestock held by an individual (herds of even a thousand or two thousand sheep are not considered very large in the American sheep-raising industry). Therefore it has been necessary for the Navajo to develop a generalized skill as herder, shepherd, cowboy, and horse wrangler in one. Being a jack-of-all-husbandry-trades has served the Navajo well, but he is often considered less than excellent when he is employed in the far more specialized husbandry of White men.

What has happened in the two hundred to two hundred and fifty years of the Navajo livestock industry is that White techniques have been borrowed and adapted to fit the Navajo situation. The basic techniques of Navajo husbandry are Spanish colonial, not Anglo–American. They were borrowed and adapted some hundred or hundred and fifty years before the Anglo–Americans in Texas began to learn the Mexican techniques of cattle- and sheep-raising, which were more use-ful in the West than were the techniques of the eastern United States. Thus, Navajo husbandry represents an independent development from basic Iberian techniques separate from and somewhat earlier than the Anglo–American development. In the last few decades the Navajo and Anglo–American traditions have become more closely associated, and the former is beginning to take on some of the specific techniques and much of the coloring of the latter.

SHEEP AND GOAT TECHNIQUES

Sheep and goats in the herd situation are generally easy to handle as long as the herder remains alert and plans what he intends to do with the herd before the leaders are committed to another action. The direction of a herd requires only that the leaders be turned, and the rest of the herd will follow. On the other hand, if a single leader gets past the turning point, the rest of the herd follows with a determination that can be thwarted only by physical restraint of the individual animals or by a fence. Thus, in the normal course of events a single herder, often a child, can watch and direct the herd grazing quite competently. But on occasions when the herd must be broken down into individuals for counting, marking, vaccinating, or shearing, the participation of every available hand is required. In such situations where the herd becomes individualized and the animals separated from each other, sheep in particular become totally confused, frightened, and unmanage-able except by manhandling. The confusion grows worse as various animals are separated from the group in the course of counting, and one feels as if he is some-how involved in keeping apart two opposite magnetic fields determined to reunite.

HERDING The primary technique for sheep herding, then, is a knowl-edge of herd behavior and an alertness to the movements of the leaders. The single herdsman may find himself in difficulty if his attention wanders too far from the herd because he may not be aware of some movement of the leaders until they are committed to a course past the possibility of being diverted. When the "sheeps get away" from the herder in this way, he can only wait until they have made their movement and then set out to extricate them from the bottom of a dead-end ravine or some such impossible place. The most common mischances on the range are when the herd moves into a space from which the leaders cannot escape without going back through the herd or when two herds drift together while grazing. The danger in the first case is that the animals cannot be induced to move before the sun is high, when they simply refuse to move and the herder must remain with them until the cooler part of the day. (This is a common occurrence when youngsters are herding sheep.) In the latter case, the two herds mingle and, in what seems almost a chemical reaction, catalyze into a single large herd. The owners must devote the rest of the day, and sometimes longer, to separating the two herds. The difficulty of this job without the aid of corrals, chutes, or pens, and with perhaps only two herders working is almost impossible to describe. It is considered one of the major and most serious inconveniences of the range. A few Navajo dogs have developed the ability to prevent such accidents by attacking the strange herd.

Sheep are timid animals, and the herder's methods are molded to fit this. Generally a herder directs the herd by simply standing up suddenly and moving in the desired direction. This usually sets the leaders off and the herd moves. Directions may be augmented with gentle sounds such as the breath expelled between the lips, low whistles, and so on. Although most families have abandoned ritual methods in sheep handling, such as the singing of a particular sheep-protecting song timed to begin with the first sheep out of the pen and to end with the last, snatches of song are often sung at this time, and one suspects that the ritual played an important role in moving sheep in the past. The song, sung regularly each morning, probably served as a signal for the easily conditioned animals to get to their feet and keep moving through the gate.

Although sheep herding seems a relatively simple task, a novice soon learns that the degree of alertness that has to be exercised is great, although the observed behavior of a Navajo herder might belie this. Despite frequent stops to watch passing hawks or eagles, a readiness to shoot a startled rabbit, or a willingness to chat with a companion, a herder is constantly watching his animals and is aware of any movements of the leaders that might commit the herd to an undesired course.

SHEEP DIPPING   On occasions when the animals must be actually controlled rather than directed, the gentle herding techniques of the range are replaced by sharply contrasting methods. Sheep dipping, which is carried out in midsummer in order to rid the sheep of ticks and other pests and partially wash excess dirt out of the wool, is a scene of frenzied activity and noise. The sheep are held in separate herds outside the pens, then moved into a holding pen where they can be examined and vaccinated. From there they are driven into chutes that terminate at the dipping vat. From the vat the animals are pushed into dripping pens, where most of the water drains onto the ground and eventually back into the vat. The greatest danger is that herds being held before or after dipping may become mixed, and, to prevent this, as many people as possible are called in to help with the herd. Standing a few feet apart, they keep the animals bunched by making a continual noise with their lips, a number of tin-can lids on a wire loop, or by beating a can or flapping a paper box. In addition, switches of brush or lariats are constantly swung toward the animals. The most difficult part of the process is moving the animals, by now terrified and confused, through the chutes and into the vats. At this point noise reaches a crescendo—tin-can rattles are shaken furiously, boxes are beaten to pieces, ropes are banged against the wood or wire fencing, animals are hit, and finally, in the last few feet, one or two people must stand in the chute literally wrestling the woolly current in the right direction as the animals panic and try to retreat down the chute in the face of their oncoming fellows. Often this leads to "plugs" of animals absolutely unable to move and requires the animal-by-animal search for the "keystone" so that the dam can be broken, the animals straightened out, and the dipping continued. Once in the pen at the mouth of the chute, the sheep are picked up and thrown into the vat, a back-breaking, finger-tearing job that requires the strongest men in the group.

Once in the vat, the sheep swim its length with the aid of women and children and a few men who stand along the sides of the vat with long crooks. In the past these poles were usually forked sticks, but in recent years these sticks have been replaced by iron piles with crooks welded on the end. The use of these crooks appears deceptively simple, but in the hands of a novice they are devices that may well drown a sheep or two. They are used properly either to push the animal down for total immersion or to lift it up and help it along the vat.

Before the dipping, the animals must be branded to identify them for the count and to prevent loss of animals in the confusion. Sheep brands are put on with paint. The usual applicator is a wire twisted into the proper shape and wrapped with wool or string to hold the paint. This is dipped into a can of commercial house paint of any color to suit the fancy of the owner, although blue and black are most common, and planted on the rump of the animal. This is a leisurely process carried out when the animals are held in the pen during the midday break. A number of people of the family lend a hand in keeping the animals bunched and in running down the ones that have escaped the brand.

SHEEPSHEARING   In the spring the wool is sheared. Until 1870 the Navajo sheared with knives, pieces of glass, tin cans, and the like. But in that year, at the suggestion of the agent, a shipment of commercial sheep shears was supplied, and these tools have entirely superseded the more primitive makeshifts. Shearing is an art understood by nearly all adults.

Sheep are usually sheared by the individual owners or, if the owners are children, by their parents, and shearing constitutes one of the few sheep operations carried out by the nuclear rather than the extended family. Goats are usually sheared first because the early prices for mohair are high. The need for cash generally forces the owner to shear at least some animals before the rest. However, there is a tendency for the family to cooperate to some degree when the major part of the herd is sheared.

In the process of shearing, the animals are thrown, tied by their ankles, and sheared, with the shearer either squatting beside the animals or standing up and bending over. The ground on which the shearing takes place is swept with a broom or some branches and a piece of canvas, if available, is spread on the ground. Hand shearing is a slow process, taking as much as an hour for a single animal, and even the most expert shearer clips the wool or hair at different lengths, thus lowering the grade of wool or mohair. Because of the danger of cutting the animal, a shearer using sheep shears usually does not cut as short as one using machine clippers, so much wool is wasted. The tribe and government have encouraged the use of machine clippers, but even the simplest of these devices is too expensive for the average Navajo.

SLAUGHTER   The slaughter of sheep is most frequently the job of women, except at a Squaw Dance when the number of animals and the demands of the cooks for mutton may force an old man to lend a hand. In slaughtering, the sheep is bound by its ankles and thrown on its side, its neck over a bucket, frying pan, or other vessel. The neck is then cut to the back bone with a short knife that would be referred to as a paring knife in a modern kitchen. The blood is drained into the vessel for use in sausage or blood pudding (the process seems always to be attended by a ring of wide-eyed little girls), and the animal is skinned and butchered. This can be done on the ground, or the animal may be hoisted by its hind legs to a limb or post. The skin is then pegged down, scraped slightly, and covered with dirt to absorb the blood and fat.

Herding cattle and horses

THE ROPE   The most important tool in handling either cattle or horses in the West is, of course, the lasso or, as it is referred to in the Southwest, the lariat or simply "rope." But there are several differences in the way it is used by the Navajo in contrast to White herdsmen. Although a few older men still make and use rawhide lariats, the most common types found today are of commercial rope of hemp or nylon. These cost from ten dollars to fifteen dollars, and often men who cannot afford these prices use makeshifts of cotton rope or other material. Navajo ropes are usually shorter than one finds in Mexico or in the West generally, in part because animals are seldom roped on the run on the open range and are therefore never more than a few feet away from the man who is trying to catch them. Cattle are seldom roped except at branding time or in order to drag a single animal into the back of a truck for transport to market. In either case, the roping is done in a corral. When it is necessary to catch grazing horses, they are most likely to be driven to nearby corrals or empty sheep pens or perhaps into a box canyon, or if several people are present, they may be simply surrounded and held. It is notable that these corrals lack a snubbing post, a post three or four feet high set in the ground in the center of the corral. These are common if not universal in corrals, particularly those used for horses, throughout the West. They allow the cowboy to rope his mount from the ground and snub his rope around the post to keep the animal from dragging him off his feet. The Navajo, as noted early in this century by the Franciscan fathers, simply allow the animal to drag them. In addition, I seldom saw a single rope being used on unbroken horses or cattle; while one member of the roping team was being dragged, others were closing in to add their ropes to the animal's neck or legs. Horses that are accustomed to being roped and ridden generally attempt to avoid the rope in the corral by milling and circling but are conditioned to stop the instant they feel a rope, whether or not it has actually encircled their neck.

Cattle are handled in much the same manner as horses. At branding time a herd is held in a pen and several Navajo cowboys on foot cut out a single animal, rope it by the neck and legs, and throw it to the ground. Once the animal is down, another man brings the branding irons from a fire outside the pen and brands the animal while the ropers hold it by leaning on the ropes.

The few occasions on which I have seen animals roped on the open range have been, to say the least, less than expert performances. On one occasion a young man, formerly a champion rodeo cowboy, roped a cow and was nearly thrown because his saddle was not cinched tight enough for roping. On yet another occasion when three Navajo and I attempted to catch and transport a range cow, the two mounted ropers lost their ropes, and the operation degenerated into a hurly-burly scramble on foot until the cow, exhausted and panic stricken (but nonetheless able to wound two of her tormentors and very nearly terminate my field investigation) was simply manhandled into a truck. Most roping is limited to rodeo performances, and the proficiency of Navajo ropers in rodeo events is not particularly great. Roping from the saddle is clearly an innovation in Navajo herding. The old-style handmade saddles that I have seen do not have a horn, which is essential for roping from the saddle. Occasionally a Navajo will rope a sheep from horseback or, in a spirit of bravado, try to rope a stray dog. Their lack of accuracy from horseback contrasts sharply with their uncanny ability on foot.

The term *cowboy* is used among the Navajo to refer, not to men who work with cattle, but to men who perform in rodeos. Methods of roping from the ground are not the same as those employed by Anglo–American or Mexican cowboys. In either of these latter traditions a man makes a loop and allows it to spread, while dragging it along the ground as he locates his target, and then launches the loop with a single overhand or side-arm motion. The Navajo, on the other hand, opens his loop and, making a few running steps, whirls the loop around his head; he depends on centrifugal force and the twisting action of the wrist to keep the loop open until he launches it with a short chopping motion of his already extended arm. Whirling a loop, of course, is characteristic of the Mexican or Anglo–American roping technique when the roper is mounted.

Cattle or horses are not generally herded on foot in the United States or Northern Mexico; they form a less compact group when moving than do sheep and move much faster, and individuals in a herd are not so loath as are sheep to quit the group and strike out on their own. Thus, although Navajo *may* herd sheep on horseback, particularly if the trip to water is a long one, they *must* herd horses and cattle while mounted. Such herding is usually done only when it is necessary to move the herd to water or from one pasture to another, and, once the trip is made, the control is removed and the animals are simply kept under periodic surveillance. The driving of cattle or horses appears to be far more relaxed among Navajo than among White cattlemen. The pace is slower, the latitude permitted individual cattle greater, and all in all the process is much more like driving a herd of sheep. Cattle are seldom, if ever, handled on the range, and if it is necessary to hold the herd while working it, the animals are run into a corral or pen. This contrasts with the Mexican and American practice of holding the herd on the open range, where mounted men continually circle, keeping the animals together while other riders cut the desired animal from the herd and drive it near the branding fire where it is roped, tied, and branded.

It should be noted that the handling of cattle by the Navajo appears in many ways to be an extension of techniques originally learned in sheep husbandry.

At the same time, younger men do not hesitate to rope a sheep or goat, an unthinkable practice by White standards.

THE BRANDING IRON   The other principal tool of the cattle herder is the branding iron, which is usually owned by the tribe. Each iron represents a letter or a number that can be applied in combination with other irons to make the individual brand. Occasionally an owner will have his own iron and will bring it to the community branding.

Since both bull calves and colts are castrated, the knowledge of the operation is essential to the keeping of livestock in this area. The technique used requires the opening of the scrotum and removal of the testes entire rather than crushing or tying the organs. The operation is performed by a specialist. One such man, an elderly gentleman who is the father of the tribal resource development chairman, is hired to work at the community brandings. In other instances, an older member of an outfit will do the castrating for all his relatives. The castrator's instruments consist of a well-sharpened penknife and a can of patent astringent powder. The fact that older, traditional males seem to have a monopoly on the operation suggests that they are perhaps considered to have horse medicine or curing power, but I observed no ritual in connection with the operation. Sheep tails are docked by applying an elastic band that allows the tail to atrophy and drop off. This practice, now nearly universal, was introduced during World War II.

RIDING AND DRIVING HORSES

THE SADDLE   Although Navajo riding increasingly tends to follow patterns found among Whites and Mexicans in the West, there are still distinctive patterns to be observed. The saddle is always the so-called Western saddle, itself a modification of Mexican stock saddles that in turn have developed from the war saddle and stock saddle brought from Spain. In the recent past the Navajo manufactured their own saddles, but this practice has been nearly abandoned. There are a few old men who still know the craft, and occasionally a homemade saddle is seen in use. The process is hedged with a number of restrictions and taboos discouraging younger men from learning the craft. Today, saddles and bridles are purchased at the trader's or from stores in Gallup, Holbrook, or Flagstaff. Saddles are usually made in the medium-low-cantled "association" style, well decorated with leather engraving and perhaps having a foam rubber seat. Old men still ride the more conservative, high-cantled, narrow-pommeled models, and almost any homestead has one or more of these models—broken and patched, with stirrups held on by rope or rawhide—which are used by women and children.

The most distinctive Navajo riding trait is one that has been noted by travelers, explorers, anthropologists, and horsemen as characteristic of most Indians of the Plains, Southwest, and Plateau-Basin areas. Compared to the American, the Navajo rides with an extremely short stirrup. In the vernacular of the West, "Indians ride like Chinamen," and in fact they do. It is far more significant perhaps that an Indian rides essentially like a Spanish soldier of the sixteenth century trained to ride *a la jineta*, the short stirrup style brought to Europe by the Moors. The difference is less marked today because younger Indians interested in rodeo events tend to lengthen their stirrups somewhat. At the same time, Western riding habits are being influenced by the "scientific" schools of European and Eastern American riding, and cowboys and rodeo performers have begun to make their own stirrups shorter than they were, let us say, half a century ago.

THE QUIRT The Navajo, like the Plains Indian but unlike the Papago and Pima, does not wear spurs. Instead he uses a quirt, and few Navajo ride far without one or without some substitute for one. This habit has given rise to statements that Indians are horse-beaters. As a matter of fact, it appears that the Navajo, at least, are seldom horse-beaters. They do keep their quirts in almost constant motion as they ride, but most of the blows fail to land, and those that do are gentle indeed. The quirt constantly urges the horse forward, substituting for the signals given with the legs or heels by White riders. In fact, many Navajo horses do not seem to respond to any leg signal save for a vigorous kick in the ribs, but work perfectly if leg signals are abandoned and a continual rain of light taps with a quirt are used. Quirts can be purchased at the trader's, and one does see them being used. However, plaited rawhide is still common, and many makeshifts such as stripped branches, sticks, rope, or strips cut from worn-out auto tires are used.

THE HOBBLE Hobbles, used to contain horses within a limited area, can also be purchased at the trader's. Homemade rawhide hobbles appear to be most common, although makeshifts of soft cotton rope are not unusual. Many Navajo do not hobble their horses but prefer to keep a horse picketed if it is necessary to keep one on hand. It is usually picketed with a short rope that prevents its grazing, and if the animal is picketed for a long time, it must be fed hay or grain or allowed to graze periodically and must be taken to water from time to time. A hobbled animal, on the other hand, can forage for itself, and the tendency is to let horses graze with hobbles at functions such as sheep dippings or dances.

MAKESHIFT EQUIPMENT Although certain items of equestrian equipment are considered necessities, the Navajo display a great willingness to use any make-shift if the choice is between riding or not. Riders using saddle blankets belted on with a surcingle,* or the surcingle alone for something to grasp in emergencies, are common sights. Almost any Navajo man will leap on a bareback horse in a situation calling for quick action, and he will ride with considerable skill. Similarly, bridles are used and considered essential, but if one is not available, it will be contrived by looping a rope over the animal's nose or through its mouth.

CARE Contrary to many popular statements about Indian cruelty or lack of concern with animal welfare, the Navajo appear to be very considerate of their horses. It must be kept in mind, however, that no amount of social symbolism alters the fact that horses in Nez Ch'ii are working livestock, maintained because they are needed from the day-to-day exigencies of existence in this isolated and virtually road-less area. Considerations for the comfort of a horse, therefore, must come after considerations of the job the animal is required to do. Horses are prized and rated according to their ability to work but certainly are never pampered with stalls,

---

* A strap that is passed around a horse to hold the saddle or saddle-pad on the animal's back.

blankets, and the other paraphernalia that are thought so essential by White pleasure-riders. Old horses are never expected to undertake a job they cannot do, but this is less from any principle of kindness than from a practical view. Pregnant mares are gradually ridden and worked less as parturition draws near. Supplemental feed is supplied to working horses, but animals not being worked must fend for themselves.

Mature animals in good condition are required to work extremely hard on occasion. The process of carrying the "stick" from the ceremonial hogan to the site of the first night of a Squaw Dance is literally a race among the younger and bolder riders, who proceed in as near a straight line as the topography will permit and as fast as possible. Sometimes this trip covers between ten and twenty miles at a lope and gallop with only brief halts to allow the horses to blow. The final morning's dash from the second night's site to the original site, which culminates in the ceremonial circling of the hogan on horseback, is equally a race. The problem of watering the overheated horses does not present itself because the animals are usually simply hobbled and turned out to graze and therefore must make their way to water rather slowly. Horses are seldom "walked cool," but after a long run such as those described above or during a rabbit hunt, the riders will pause for a few moments to chat and dismount while the animals cool off before proceeding to water.

It is common to strip the saddle at this time and bathe the horse whenever the water hole is of sufficient size to permit it. For the rider who still has some way to ride before he can unsaddle, the alternative is to ride his mount up to its belly into a pond or dam.

After a hard run, the horses are turned out to graze and allowed to rest for several days. During this period the animals are stiff and sore and their muscles work unwillingly, and the Navajo usually avoids using the horse at such times unless it is absolutely necessary. Such practices are clearly related to a time when the individual Navajo had many more horses available than he has today, when the periods of rest for a tired horse caused no inconvenience because other animals were available. Today these same patterns are maintained, sometimes with the result that for several days after a Squaw Dance or rabbit hunt a horse owner must walk. It should be noted that the occasions of greatest effort for horses are related to social or religio–social events such as rabbit hunts, Squaw Dances, and rodeos. In actual work on the range, horses are used rather gently. Because cattle are seldom roped on the range, the hard usage often accorded White cow horses is avoided, and the most that is demanded of the Navajo cow pony is only occasional short bursts of speed. Generally, herding methods are so relaxed as compared to White techniques that horses seldom get out of a walk.

The most common gait for Navajo horses is either a rather long swinging walk or lope. This pattern is the same throughout the West and wherever the basic equestrian techniques are Spanish. The trot is a difficult and uncomfortable gait to ride unless the rider posts, and posting, which was in fact developed for riding on roads, has its disadvantages in rough country. The lope, which is no faster but much more comfortable for both horse and rider, is used whenever a Navajo is traveling any distance.

Navajo women ride often and well, although perhaps not as vigorously as the men. The only general concession to sex is that a blanket is often thrown over the saddle when a woman rides. This serves as a decoration but also protects a woman's legs and inner thighs from chafing.

TRAINING   Training of horses is gradual and informal. Colts and fillies run with their dams until weaning. They follow adult horses when they are ridden or driven and become completely accustomed to the presence of human beings. It is common to see colts lying asleep by their dams who are still harnessed to the wagon and waiting to be driven home from a Squaw Dance, while hundreds of people walk, dance, and sing within a few feet of them. As a colt begins to get its growth, the process of breaking is undertaken rather informally by young boys. Already used to humans, the animal generally does not resist when youngsters climb on it and ride for short distances. Such early mounting does not seem to have adverse effects on the development of the back because the riders are light and the periods of mounting short. By the time the horse has reached full growth, it is already "green broken"—that is, used to having riders on its back and not likely to buck vigorously. The horse is taught to accept the process of saddling and bridling and learns to respond to rein signals.

Training beyond the elementary stages is not generally undertaken except by young men interested in competing in rodeos. The two classes of competition requiring a trained horse are roping and bulldogging. Navajo horses do not seem to be particularly well trained as roping horses. The primary requirement in roping is that the horse must remain facing the roped animal and must back away, keeping the rope taut and preventing the calf from regaining its feet while the rider dismounts and ties the calf's feet. Of the several dozen roping horses I saw during my stay, only a few were able to carry out this part of the job with any degree of efficiency. Training for this skill appears to be based first on an observed talent in the horse for such work and then by the rider's roping from the animal in the hope that practice will somehow make it perfect. Bulldogging requires a horse to run straight and very close to the target steer so that the rider can lean forward and grasp the animal's horns before leaving the saddle. It was my impression that the number of animals that jibbed (swerved off course), causing their riders to miss altogether and sprawl face down in the dust, was considerably higher than one sees in White rodeos.

Beyond this, very little specialized training is required of any Navajo horse. Most horses can be driven as well as ridden; however, a particularly good riding horse is usually not driven, and there are always a few horses that drive calmly but react violently when ridden.

The Navajo are particularly fond of horse racing, and a fast horse may be kept largely for that purpose. Most racing is informal, and matches are often made at Squaw Dances. Some rodeos have more formal competitions, usually half-mile dashes. Young light riders mounted bareback or with only a surcingle often serve as jockeys.

Although any horse may be pressed into service on a rabbit hunt, certain animals show a distinct talent for spotting rabbits and following them closely without direction from the rider, much as a good polo pony becomes accustomed to following the ball. Such animals are prized, but no special training methods are used to develop such talent.

ATTITUDE TOWARD FALLING   One significant aspect of Navajo horsemanship is the casualness with which a fall from a horse is accepted. Among White riders a fall is considered a sign of inexpertness, and although it will be laughed off by the one who falls, it is nonetheless not taken lightly. Experienced riders tend to minimize falls with statements like "If you haven't been pitched off a few times, you're not a rider."

The Navajo, on the other hand, do not seem so concerned with a fall as a sign of inexpertness. The willingness to ride whatever horse happens to be available, with or without saddle, and the abandon with which such activities as rabbit hunting and racing are carried out means that falls are to be expected, and they are frequent. On one rabbit hunt, for instance, in which eight adults were riding, there were four falls in the course of an hour—exclusive of the rather spectacular fall I had. All the riders were experienced and skillful and had been riding since childhood. It was clear that no one felt such falls were signs of inexperience but simply part of the expected course of events. It was equally clear, however, that a fall had to be treated lightly by the man who fell. One of the few occasions on which I witnessed a Navajo child being struck was when a twelve-year-old boy refused to get up after he fell from a horse and instead lay on the ground sobbing.

THE TEAM   All Navajo appear to know how to drive a team and hitch it to a wagon. However, such work is usually performed by men if any are present. No particular driving skill is displayed or required today in the Nez Ch'ii area because the hitches are limited to a simple two-horse hitch, and the pace is either a walk or a very slow trot.

Harness is purchased from traders, as are wagons. However, the price of a wagon and harness, presently about five hundred dollars, has led to a high degree of expertness and ingenuity in repairing and maintaining this equipment. Harness is most often repaired with rawhide or, in recent times, with strips cut from old automobile tires and riveted together.

Wagons are repaired with scrap lumber; worn wheels are rounded out with strips of rubber tires and re-tired in iron. Often nothing of the original wagon remains except the metal work, hub, and felloes.* On some part of the reservation many wagons are constructed from an auto or truck chassis, wheels, and tires, but these are uncommon in the Nez Ch'ii area largely because they are too low to negotiate the rough wagon tracks in this region. All wagons can be fitted with bows† and covered to keep off the sun, and they usually are when used to transport people or livestock. The cover is removed for hauling wood, barrels of water, or brush for the roofing and siding of shades.

COMMERCIAL COMPETITION   In the past, saddles and bridles were made of rawhide, and Navajo smiths fabricated bits. However, bit making seems to have disappeared in the face of the competition of manufactured articles. Some Navajo

* Shaped wooden rims of the wheels.
† Curved wooden slats used to support a canvas cover on a wagon.

silversmiths still make ornate silver-decorated headstalls for on-reservation sale and for sale to White tourists, but they are expensive and few Navajo can afford them.

Saddle blankets are often old bedding, but many people, particularly on festive occasions, use Navajo saddle blankets. This is the only domestic use of Navajo weaving. A few old men still cherish buffalo-hide saddle blankets, and, for their part, a few young men prize factory-made saddle pads.

VETERINARIAN SKILLS The most common ills of the horse—those involving strains and bruises of the feet and legs, stone bruises of the frog (the elastic horny pad in the sole of the foot, splints (a bony enlargement on the upper part of the cannon bone), and bowed or strained tendons—are difficult to treat under any circumstances, and among the Navajo they usually appear to be left for time to heal. A horse disabled in this manner is generally turned out to rest and not worked until it improves. However, most Navajo men know a traditional form of treatment for "knocked" shoulder that demands a degree of surgical skill, inasmuch as it requires incisions to drain off surplus fluid that collect between the flesh and the hide. Most Navajo men also claim competence in removing lampers, the horny growths that often develop in the roof of a horse's mouth when the diet contains large amounts of rough or thorny matter. The fact that both these operations are described by the Franciscan Fathers indicates that knowledge of them is not particularly recent. For more severe injuries the Navajo have recourse to the same curing techniques traditionally available to humans—curers with supernaturally sanctioned powers. These men form a loosely organized association of horse doctors sharing esoteric and ritual knowledge concerning the treatment of horses. During my stay in the area, one horse was severely injured in the ceremonies on the third morning of a Squaw Dance. The animal ran into the ceremonial hogan, which had been hurriedly constructed and had a number of snags jutting from it, one of which tore a large wound in the animal's shoulder. The blood was staunched by the application of mud, and then the animal was turned over to several men reported to know how to cure horses.

HUNTING

Hunting is discussed here because it has such a close relationship to livestock husbandry. Hunting is actually only a sport among the people of Nez Ch'ii, although the game taken may constitute a welcome and sometimes essential addition to the diet. However, hunting is justified by them in terms of its relation to agriculture and animal husbandry as well as being simply "fun."

In the past fifty years deer have been hunted in the mesa tops in the northern part of this region, but it has been many years since any have been reported.

Bears are still fairly common in the Lukachukai Mountains, but none have been reported for many years in the Nez Ch'ii area. Thus, the only game in the area is limited to two species of rabbits—cottontail and jackrabbit—prairie dogs, and a number of smaller predators.

Rabbits are taken in mounted hunts by means of sticks hurled at them by the pursuing riders. Such hunts are primarily social in nature, and informants state that since the inception of rodeo contests a few years ago, such hunts have become smaller and are held less often because the daring young riders prefer rodeos to rabbit chasing. The recreational aspect of such a hunt is quite clear in the English sentence, "Some boys are coming over tomorrow and we gonna have fun." However, the hunts are also justified in terms of the damage that rabbits do the corn fields, and they are held most frequently during the period when the corn is most easily damaged. When the snow in the winter is about three inches deep, impeding rabbits but not horses, rabbit hunts are also regularly staged.

Prairie-dog hunting was, until the population of these animals was reduced, common and popular, particularly with boys' and young men, who lured them into the opening of their dens with a mirror and killed them with a barbed arrow. The hunters also took them by waiting near a "town" and shooting them with small caliber rifles.

In the winter, wildcats are tracked in the snow and shot, as are badger and fox if they are encountered. These winter hunts are described as "real fun" but justified, in addition, in terms of the potential damage these animals, particularly the wildcat, may do to sheep herds.

Many birds are killed, but seldom for food. Eagles are taken whenever they are encountered because of their value in Navajo ritual. An eagle skin with all the feathers is worth about twenty-five dollars. Bluebirds and owls also can be sold alive or dead to medicine men. Buzzards are shot at for sport, and a species of jay is killed because "it pecks at the corn." A variety of large swallow (bize) is occasionally killed in the summer because the act is said to bring rain.

UTILITY FOR LIVESTOCK OPERATIONS One important function of the hunting complex and of the avid interest in hunting and killing animals displayed by most Navajo men and boys in that it trains Navajo males in a number of skills of singular importance to their livestock-raising activity.

Successful livestock operations in this area require an extremely detailed knowledge of a relatively limited area. The location of springs, seeps, and wells must be known, as well as sites of potentially good grazing and places where stock might become confused or lost. This knowledge could theoretically be gained from observation during actual herding operations or from more formal instruction. However, the amount of time spent with the herd by any one youth is a relatively small part of his life, considering the system of rotation of duty that exists within the homestead group. The remainder of his waking time is usually devoted to the pursuit of animals of all sorts and sizes with a sling-shot made of inner tube, a crude bow and arrow, or perhaps an ancient small-caliber gun that is usually kept secreted in a cave or tree out of sight of adults. This constant hunting develops the required knowledge that will later be put to good use in tending livestock.

Moreover, hunting develops the Navajo skill of tracking animals on the often dry, hard, and unyielding soil, a skill that is essential to the successful conduct of livestock operations on an open range. The ability of Navajo men and boys to follow the track of a single jackrabbit over ground recently churned by horses, perpetually marked by sheep hooves, and traced and retraced by numerous other jackrabbits is truly amazing. This skill is often put to the test in tracing down stray horses and cattle or seeking out lost sheep. The ability not only to follow a trail but also to identify a particular animal's hoof print is a requirement for any Navajo herder. Thus, the combined knowledge of terrain and tracking that is developed by boys and men is essential to their livestock operation, conducted as it is without fences on overcrowded but extremely rugged range. To some degree women share this knowledge, but it seldom appears to be as highly developed in them as it is in males. Nonetheless, most Navajo women are what we might term "track conscious" and seldom miss any obvious signs left in the earth by passing animals or humans. A Navajo woman was able to give a fairly accurate account of my own wanderings on foot and horseback from her observation of my week-old tracks.

RITUAL BEHAVIOR Aboriginal hunting was highly and rigidly ritualized and has been described in much detail by Hill. Today, much if not all of this ritual is absent in hunts staged by Navajo men. However, certain behavior that I observed reflects the ritual strictures of aboriginal life.

In keeping with the mythological view that wild animals and man are products of the same act of creation, that animals once shared language, culture, and society with man, and that today they offer themselves as a volunteer sacrifice to man, no animal was killed without reason during my stay. Whenever an animal was killed, or an attempt was made to kill one, a reason was offered. Jackrabbits were killed to be eaten or fed to the dogs or because they ate the corn; bluejays were killed because they could be sold to a medicine man or because they picked the corn. An owl could be used to supply arrow feathers. A swallow killed in midsummer would bring rain. On one occasion my companion, who usually carried a rifle, stopped to shoot a buzzard. The act was quite without justification, as buzzards are inedible and their feathers are useful only in a single ceremonial context. Nonetheless my friend claimed, until he had fired and startled the bird into flight, that he was shooting at an eagle, extremely valuable for arrow feathers and in ceremonies. I am sure that his sudden lack of discernment was simply a cover to allow him to shoot at a living creature for pleasure.

Certain animals such as the coyote and the rattlesnake are not supposed to be killed because of their supernatural power. In conversations with Navajo men about hunting, it was pointed out that despite these ritual prohibitions both the coyote and rattlesnake were regularly killed *because they were a threat to humans and livestock*. In other areas where black bear are common and a threat to sheep, the Navajo, wherever possible, ask a White trader to kill the marauder in order to escape any possibility of revenge by the bear spirit. Members of the various deer clans are reluctant to kill deer or eat venison except on special occasions.

It is interesting in light of the reported behavior toward wild animals to note the casualness with which a wandering dog is killed or shot at. No explanation or excuse was ever offered for killing a stray dog. Nor is there any ceremony involved in the slaughter of a sheep or goat. The job is done in a casual manner, usually by two women who gossip and joke while they quickly slit the animal's throat and proceed to butcher the carcass.

Another stricture of Navajo hunting ritual required hunters to concentrate entirely on hunting. Only hunting was discussed, dreams of blood and killing were hoped for, and hunters were cautioned to keep their thoughts on the job at hand.

Today there is no formalized requirement for such concentration, but actual behavior follows the pattern closely. When a group of men have decided to hold a rabbit chase and have ridden away from the homestead, hunting dominates their thoughts and conversation. They discuss the hunt to come, where rabbits may be lying, rabbits they have seen recently, past hunts, the virtue of their horses as rabbit-chasers, whether or not the sticks they have cut are good rabbit clubs, and so forth. After each chase each detail of the run is discussed and analyzed over and over again. Any attempt to introduce some other subject into the conversation is either ignored or curtly rejected.

On one occasion I had ridden into the mesas with two brothers to search for owls to provide arrow feathers. In the course of our search we had casually killed a number of bluejays (because they picked the corn) and one cottontail (for dinner). Moving into the flatlands again, the brothers decided to have a rabbit chase. The casual air of the trip suddenly evaporated as we cut sticks and spread out in line. The chase ended successfully after less than two minutes. The discussion of the chase continued without interruption for the next thirty minutes until we had dismounted at the homestead.

The contrast between the single-mindedness of a hunter and the apparent casualness of the same man when herding sheep is interesting. Although always alert to the movement of the herd, the shepherd willingly discusses any subject that crosses his mind, engages in target shooting, undertakes brief stalks after rabbits (with the attendant critique of rabbit behavior), or simply enjoys nature.

LEARNING THE TECHNIQUES OF HERDING

One might draw a comparison between the cultural and individual foundation of livestock herding among the Navajo. The livestock culture of today rests on the aboriginal hunting-and-gathering culture of the past, and in the same way the individual's basic knowledge of herding skills depends to a significant degree on the hunting for its continuation. However, there are many details of livestock herding that must be learned directly by young Navajo. This section will deal with the methods of teaching employed.

Because children are required to assume herding responsibilities somewhere between their eighth and tenth year, the skills must be taught early and taught well enough for youngsters to be entrusted with the herd with a fairly high degree of confidence.

Just as Navajo horse training is rather unstructured and informal, so is the training of Navajo children to work with animals. Most of the herding skills are developed as part of childhood play and not through any formal teaching programs.

The children live in a world very close to animals. The house or hogan is seldom more than a few dozen or hundred yards from the sheep pen or the horse corral. A horse is often tied from dawn to sunset within a few yards of the hogan, and the ubiquitous dog is constantly present. Toddlers less than two years old are apt to attempt to ride a dog or wrestle it and pull its ears until it flees. Chickens receive the same kind of attention from tiny children, although they are seldom incautious enough to fall into an infant's grip. Thus, children grow up with little or no fear of animals, and by the time they are two years old they fearlessly confront any stray sheep, goat, or cow that comes near, with shouts and arm wavings. They soon learn that most animals react quickly to such demonstrations. Certainly before their first birthday they have been taken up on the saddle by their father or an uncle and already experienced their first horseback ride.

EARLY INITIATION By the time a child is three, he or she is allowed to participate in herding activities about the homestead. While one or two adults and several older children handle the sheep as they are being marked in the pen, children of three, four, and five are also in the pen "helping." Although their misguided and enthusiastic pursuit of sheep often hinders the operation, they are seldom made to stop, nor are they corrected. After a time an older child may take over the task of moving a sheep toward the marker and thus leave a youngster in screaming frustration. Only if there is real danger would a child be forcibly removed from the pen. In fact, children so young as to be clumsy on their feet may be used in herding when their father, uncle, or older brother places them on the ground at some gap in the sheep-pen fence; from that position, they serve to drive away the animals seeking to escape while the herd is being handled for one reason or another.

In herding it is quite common for the sheep to be allowed simply to drift into the pen by force of habit after they have been brought within a few hundred yards of the homestead. (A herd is often spoken of as "good" if it finds its way home without straggling.) If they desire, four- and five-year-olds may then take over the task of penning the sheep. Imitating their elders as best they can and often forced to combine forces to pull a stubborn ram by his horns until he faces the right direction, the youngsters drive the animals to the pen and close the gate. The adults appear to pay no attention to these efforts but do covertly watch to prevent the youngsters' enthusiasm from starting a stampede.

By the time a boy or girl has reached six or seven, he or she may accompany the herder with the herd onto the range, particularly if the herder is one of the older children, but seldom if the herder is an adult other than a parent.

THE ROPE Toys are few in a Navajo household and those few are shared by all the children in the homestead. Girls usually have manufactured dolls, but boys' toys are most often makeshifts, the most common and most prized of which is a piece of rope fashioned into a lariat. From about the age of three, roping practice begins, usually with a piece of string and shifting, and continues, as the boy's expertness and discrimination develops, with the best rope he can find. Youngsters rope continually, using any object as a target, including dogs, chickens, sheep, each other, and younger siblings. Navajo children are generally retiring with strangers, and even when they have become friendly they may lapse into dumbness if suddenly confronted with a direct question about themselves. However, boys are invariably eager to show their skill with a rope.

Skill with a rope is an important factor in establishing one's prestige in early manhood. Almost without exception, boys and young men yearn to participate in rodeos in which calf roping is considered, along with saddle bronc riding, as an honored event. A family that includes a male who has a reputation as a "cowboy" basks in his glory, and his status as a "cowboy" far outweighs any other accomplishments he may possess.

Because roping is by and large a technique of cattle herding, it is less commonly a skill of women, although most women appear capable of lassoing a horse in a corral. However, so ubiquitous is the "roping complex" that a woman preparing a meal may fashion a loop in a piece of string and casually lasso a pot or a pan and drag it to her rather than rise or even lean forward to get it.

PLAY   The most common games played by Navajo children are those involving an imitation of herding activities. Older siblings willingly play horse for toddlers. Older children frequently draft younger siblings as "horses" to be led by a rope. The family wagon is a focus of much play whenever it is not in use. Two children play the role of horses, pawing, snorting, and buck jumping, displaying considerably more spirit than the average Navajo team, while another serves as driver for the rest of the children crowded into the wagon bed. At other times somewhat older children will pair off and play bucking bronco, or one will take a rope in his or her mouth while the partner "drives."

RIDING   Learning to ride is a gradual process, progressing from being taken up on the pommel by a father, uncle, or older brother to riding behind an adult or older child until, between nine and twelve, a child begins to ride the less fractious horses by himself. In fact, he seldom is completely alone because the youngsters' demand for animals to ride far exceeds the supply. A boy almost always has a younger sibling or cousin riding behind him, or two boys of about the same age ride and walk alternately. In their early teens, boys generally take over the job of driving horses that have been penned at night to water. A strict precedence of age is observed in carrying out this popular job, which usually permits a bit of galloping and rope waving. Before he is completely entrusted with this job, usually in his twelfth year, a boy is often taken on rides by his father or uncle. Although these rides are seemingly casual, the older man is carefully watching the boy's behavior. Not infrequently the trip includes a ride to the top of a high mountain or past some sacred spot. Generally such trips end in a "race," with the son's being allowed to ride the better horse and win. Once trusted to ride off by himself on horseback, a boy is considered an adult. It is at this time he receives a lariat, often purchased at no little sacrifice. It is also the time when he is given a horse if it is at all possible. He is no longer expected to come home every night and is felt to be old enough to cope with the dangers of large gatherings—that is, he is expected to take care of himself in the presence of drunken people.

Girls sometimes ride when they herd sheep, and if no older boy is present to herd the horses, they may occasionally take over the job. However, they ride for "fun" whenever they can. They take advantage of the special brother–sister relationship to importune their brothers, a situation that often results in a Navajo boy's walking home from some function to which he had ridden because he could not in good conscience deny his sister the use of the horse. However, female ambition in equestrian skills is thwarted by a lack of opportunity for expression. Older teen-age girls are faced with a choice of marriage on-reservation, the possibility of employment on-reservation, or of going off-reservation to seek employment; in any case, their ability as expert riders is not significant beyond their riding well enough to help with the herding. Rarely, a girl enters in one of the gymkhana classes of the rodeo such as the barrel race. This is not considered entirely good behavior by the Navajo, and such entrants are more likely to be Hopi girls.

By the time a Navajo child has reached his or her late teens, all the basic skills of livestock handling have been acquired. Special skills such as horseshoeing, operating for lampers or hide-bound shoulders, vaccinating, castrating, and de-horning may or may not be learned in adult life. Relatively few Navajo in this area shoe their horses since it is cheaper to rest a horse with sore feet than to purchase commercially made horseshoes or even, assuming the possession of the skill, to buy iron for making horseshoes.

Ownership, Benefit, and Responsibility

Livestock raising in the Nez Ch'ii area is often a family or communal enter-prise, but actual title of each animal is retained by an individual. The ultimate right to alienate any animal rests with the person considered to be the animal's owner. There are distinct patterns of ownership in the various classes of livestock, and perhaps more important than ownership is the benefit from the sale or slaughter of an animal. Many people besides the owner are involved in the care of the utilitarian and marketable animals, and many people besides him receive some share of the income.

Moreover, with certain classes of livestock there *is* an element of communal ownership involved. An individual Navajo will identify all the animals in a herd as "his" when he is speaking in general terms but if pressed for details will break down the herd according to the members of the group who actually hold title to the individual animals. It should be remembered that this is a social rather than a legal title. The institution of the grazing-permit system created a number of special problems inasmuch as permits were issued to individuals, although the herd may have in fact belonged to a number of people. Occasionally single animals are considered as jointly owned, but this situation is rare and may be limited in application to horses, or perhaps cattle, purchased with pooled funds. Only once did I hear an animal referred to as belonging to more than one person; this was a horse, and it belonged to a sister of the informant and her husband. The animal may have belonged in fact solely to the husband, but there is a strong tendency to identify a sister's husband with the sister and make claims on her property through her.

SHEEP AND GOATS

The sheep and goat herd usually is composed of animals owned by the individuals of a matrilineal group—that is, a woman, her daughters and sons, and perhaps even her brothers who live elsewhere with their wives. A husband may, if he wishes, buy sheep or bring sheep to be added to the herd at the time of his marriage. These sheep do not constitute a marriage payment but remain his property. However, a payment in sheep and jewelry is usually made to the bride's parents.

Children are usually given sheep and goats by their father, although his brothers or their mother's brothers may also give them sheep. The occasion for such gifts is in the spring during lambing season. In addition, a husband will often make his wife a present of several lambs at this time. Once the gift has been made to a child, the adults defer to the child on the question of disposing of the animal.

Every effort is made to save the sheep belonging to a boy or girl so that each child will have the beginning of a herd of his own when he or she is old enough to marry. However, when older children go to off-reservation schools for long periods and cannot contribute to the care of the herd, their animals are not infrequently slaughtered for food. The rationale seems to be that this is recompense for having cared for the animals while the owner was away. This is not always considered unfavorably by younger Navajo who have been educated. The lack of sheep relieves them of the arduous task of herding when they are home on vacation.

Responsibility for sheep and goats, however, is clearly that of the entire homestead group. The duty of herding the sheep is rotated from adult to adult when there are enough adults. If not, young adults and children either share the responsibility as helpers or assume full responsibility if adults are busy with other chores. It seems equally clear that liability for the sheep herd is shared by all the homestead group, and when the herd does not come home as expected, the entire group becomes concerned and begins to search. However, the members most closely related to the herder usually start searching first and continue longer than the other members of the group.

Jobs such as counting and dipping the sheep require the active participation of the entire homestead group. Some members must make the drive with the sheep and camp near the vat to hold the herd at night. Others remain at home until morning and then join the herders at the vat to assist in handling the sheep. At the same time, at least one adult woman or older girl must remain at the homestead to watch the infants and toddlers who do not go to the dipping.

When an animal is slaughtered for food, it is the property of a single individual but at the same time is shared with everyone present. Slaughtering for food seems to follow an informal rotation so that each individual suffers about the same drain on his or her holdings. If, however, as sometimes happens, one of the family comes home with a mutton hunger and demands meat, one of his animals will be killed. If he returns home to get meat to take away from the homestead and not to share with the rest of the group, it is his sheep that will be slaughtered.

The sale of sheep is also an individual activity. Members of the group select stock from among their own animals to sell at a time that is convenient to them. The proceeds of such sales are the property of the seller.

CATTLE

Cattle are much less a group enterprise. Women by and large show little interest in cattle operations, although occasionally a woman may buy a calf to raise. Cattle handling is considered to be a man's job and one that women cannot or will not do. More often than not, the cattle belonging to a homestead are the particular property and concern of one or two men of the group. Although the group will assume general responsibility for the animals, such as seeing that they are watered, it is up to the owner to find them if they are lost, to round them up and herd them to branding, and to assist in the branding. He may have the help of a brother-in-law or brother, particularly if he has a younger brother who is interested in being a "cowboy," but such help is considered a favor and in some way should be repaid.

Proceeds from cattle sales are the property of the owner of the cattle. The close relationship of Navajo brothers and sisters usually means that a man can count on a sister to look after his cattle interests if he has to leave home to work.

The distinctly different attitudes evidenced toward sheep and cattle are the foci of a pervading conflict in homesteads of the Nez Ch'ii area. Many young men who object to the demands placed on them by the sheep—the continual care, the repeated penning, the duty of herding—and who are conscious that for the past decade cattle have been the more profitable enterprise want to give up sheep husbandry and concentrate exclusively on cattle. However, women—wives, sisters, and mothers—and the more traditional men resist such moves vigorously. This resistance is probably due to the women's important role in sheep husbandry as herders, butchers, and shearers; they can handle sheep in the course of their domestic duties, and the wool from the sheep also provides them with material for rugs, which often constitute an important income source. If sheep were abandoned, women would no longer have such a central place in the economic system, and in all probability their overall influence and security would be weakened. For instance, no Navajo woman need endure mistreatment, or even boredom, from a husband because she is economically unable to leave him or, more properly, to order him to leave. A shift to cattle economy would place the economic reins more fully in his hands because even if she owned the cattle, it would be essential that a man be available to herd them.

HORSES

Horses are owned individually but they are shared within the homestead group. There is an informal but seldom violated precedence of horse usage, with the owner always having first choice of riding the animal he owns. In his absence or with his acquiescence, the riding privilege descends to his brothers and sisters, then to their spouses, then to other more distant relatives, and finally to the younger children who operate according to a precedence of age without reference to near-ness of relationship. However, the rights of the owner must sometimes be tempered by the welfare of the homestead group, and his horse must be hitched to the wagon even though he would like to go on a ride or search for his cattle. Nevertheless, if he should insist on his right, the entire group will acquiesce, displaying only a very restrained resentment, and wait until he is through with the animal. This precedence of ownership does not extend to the children if actual title rests in a child, which is not infrequent. Having received a horse from his father, a boy may experience several years of frustration while his father usurps the animal and the use precedence descends from his father through the adults until it finally shifts into the children's system where the "owner" may have precedence if he can prevail over the demands of the older boys and his demanding sisters.

PRESSURES TOWARD COLLECTIVITY

The individualistic tendencies in stock ownership are clearly tempered by the dependence on others that is so essential for survival. The decision to sell stock or slaughter sheep is not completely unilateral and seldom is made without informal conferences. At the very least, such decisions are usually made with the knowledge that the action will not be greatly resisted by others.

How strong these collective pressures on the individual are can best be illustrated by the case of Crooked Fingers, who is thirty-eight, seldom refused by his family or in-laws, and tends to be charmingly overbearing. He is consumed with a desire to raise cattle, but in his own words, "My mother and sister won't let me." This female opposition prevents him from buying more cattle openly. However, he often buys calves secretly and gives them to friends to keep for him. When his mother and older sister left the reservation to weed and harvest crops in Idaho, he immediately began to bring his calves into the homestead knowing that economic prudence would prevent the women from taking any action to remove these valuable animals when confronted with a fait accompli. His scheming was not impeded by his adoring younger sister, although she was fully aware that the other women would be angry when they returned.

The Family and the Herd

The relationship between the family and the herd is one tinged with rather deep emotion and a great deal of symbolism. Sheep are not only wealth in an objective sense but serve as a measure of family well-being on a more abstract level of discourse. One is quickly impressed with the identification between "the family" and the "sheep."

This is most clearly seen whenever any unusual activity with the herd is planned. Thus dipping, shearing, shifting of pastures, or emergencies such as droughts, during which water is hauled to the herd, require the presence of as many members of the family as possible. Never are all the members pressed into service. Nonetheless, while those actually working the herd are busy, the others remain standing or sitting nearby carefully watching the operation. Often the preparation of meals is delayed while the women sit near the sheep pen watching the men bring the animals out to water. In fact, it would be considered somewhat less than proper if one of the women did not join the others at a time like this. At sheep dippings, members of the family not resident at the homestead usually appear to assist the family casually and to talk to their relatives. This is most often done in the sheep pen or near it. On several different occasions Navajo living at a distance from the family home where the sheep were kept asked me to drive them there, and in most instances the reason they gave for wanting to take the trip was to "see the sheep." "I haven't seen the sheep for a long time" was considered sufficient explanation for wanting to visit one's homestead. On one occasion, having taken a woman and her husband to visit one of her sisters, we found that the sheep were still grazing. After waiting for perhaps an hour we were forced to leave before the herd was brought in because of a sudden snow storm. The woman's complaint, "I sure wanted to see them sheep," could be compared only to a White relative who had missed seeing a favorite niece or nephew during a visit.

Quite often, particularly in the winter and spring, the sheep pen serves as a center of social intercourse for the women of a family. Generally keeping to their hogans in the daytime, they emerge some time before the herd is due to return and assemble in the sheep pen. There they fondle the lambs (and their children, quite without distinction) and discuss the affairs of the day, all the while holding hands, caressing each other casually, or otherwise expressing the Navajo trait of tactile assurance in face-to-face interpersonal relationships. This period is looked forward to all through the day as a time of relaxation and gratification and, even under the most miserable of weather conditions, is a time of gentle laughter and joking. When the sheep arrive, the women help herd them into the pen and assist the lambs in finding their dams before dispersing to prepare the evening meal.

However, when the family is torn by interpersonal tensions or openly expressed hostilities for any reason, the care of the sheep herd drops off noticeably. The animals are simply turned out of the pens and left to fend for themselves, with only a casual watch being kept. As often as not, they will not be driven to water until necessity forces the move. Once penned in the late morning, they may not be taken out in the afternoon at all. The job of herding may be assigned entirely to children, with an attendant series of derelictions. In short, as a focus of cooperation the sheep herd serves as a means of expressing both affection and hostility toward one's close relatives. It also serves as an anchor for members of the family not normally resident. Such relatives may periodically come back to the family homestead and insist on herding the sheep for a few days, thus establishing their relationship symbolically as well as creating an obligation on the part of the family. School-age boys often insist on herding sheep during the last few days of their summer vacation. On one occasion a young man came all the way from a summer job in Wyoming to spend a few days with his family before the school year started. In those few days he spent a goodly part of his time with the sheep on the range. Similarly, his older brother, who is employed by the Bureau of Indian Affairs, spends most of his vacation periods herding sheep at the family homestead.

These are examples of behavior, emanating from an attitude that is clear but difficult to describe, that links the sheep herd to the matrilineal family. Extremely old men point with pride to animals in the herd that are descended from the original animals issued by the government after Fort Sumner. Families will tell with pride how their immediate ancestor or ancestress began life with only a few sheep but increased the herd through perseverance, the proper exercise of ritual power, and right living.

The word *love* is used frequently to describe a Navajo's feeling toward his sheep. To quote from a letter written by one of my informants, "It's hard to make a living out here with our sheeps and cattles but we love them and will keep on trying no matter how hard it is."

Many observers of the Navajo have commented that in large part their resentment of the stock reduction program was a result of the government's allowing thousands of sheep to die in holding pens or en route to the railroads. Such behavior, perfectly understandable in White economic terms, was viewed as utter barbarism by the Navajo and is still spoken of in Nez Ch'ii. The fact that lambs, kids, and colts running with their mothers were worth nothing to stock reduction buyers was keenly resented not only in economic terms, but also as an insult to the persons of the animals.

Thus the Navajo is linked to his herds both in a simple economic relationship and by deep emotional ties in which he and his family's continuity and well-being, as well as his own self-image, are symbolized by his herds.

7

The Crops

THE NAVAJO learned to farm from the Pueblo peoples and adopted the native crops of corn, beans, pumpkins, melons, and squash that had been developed in the New World. They were also quick to adopt European crops such as peaches, oats, wheat, and barley. Except in a few well-watered areas, the Navajo were never enthusiastic farmers. Herds of animals, not large fields, constituted the basis of wealth and prestige.

In the Nez Ch'ii area, farming is particularly difficult. Rain is infrequent and unpredictable. There is never any certainty of making a crop. Water sources are too limited and uncertain to permit the development of irrigation.

Nonetheless, every homestead group works one or more fields to supplement its diet. Unlike the herd, which is tended communally, the cornfield is spoken of and managed as the individual project of a nuclear family. It is always identified with the wife rather than the husband, especially if the couple have taken up matrilocal residence. Occasionally two sisters may join efforts on a single field. This is particularly true if one of them is widowed or separated.

The common crops are corn, squash, and pumpkin. Regular efforts are made to maintain peach trees, but usually the seedling plants die from lack of water or from being stripped by grazing sheep. Occasional and sometimes successful attempts are made to grow potatoes, but the uncertainty of moisture often brings about failure. In as many as one out of three years even the cornfield fails to produce a crop because of lack of rain. Nonetheless, each year the crop is put in and the land worked in hope.

Fields are usually located on the traditional use area of the homestead group but often as much as several miles from the home of the farmer. At different periods of intense activity a brush shelter may be built near the field so that the nuclear unit can camp there to avoid a long round trip each day.

In the past the Navajo were noted for planting their fields in a peculiar spiral plan. However, with the introduction of the plough, after the return from Fort Sumner, this system was abandoned and with it much of the ritual associated with agriculture. The land is turned in the late spring after the snow has melted but hopefully while at least some moisture remains in the soil. Because no fertilizer is used, the fields quickly exhaust themselves, so that new ones have to be cleared by ploughing and burning every two or three years. The corn seeds are planted very deeply and very widely spaced and with them the seeds of watermelon, pumpkin, and squash. Once planted, there is little more that can be done save warding off birds that might steal the seeds before they sprout. If the rains are adequate, there may be some weed development that requires work in the midsummer. Frequently rain is so lacking that the corn stalks stand for weeks without apparent growth in fields absolutely barren of any other plants. If late summer rains come and are not so heavy as to wash out the field altogether, the almost dormant crops suddenly begin to mature, and by early September—late August in some places, October in others—the crops are ready for harvest.

The Navajo diet is singularly lacking in fresh vegetables, and many recipes for preparing unripe corn and pumpkins have been developed. In this way the farmer need not wait until the end of the growing season for vegetables and is also able to salvage something of a crop that has failed to mature completely. Roast green corn ears are extremely popular, as are green pumpkins, sliced and boiled in deep fat. Because the climate in this area is so inconsistent, crops in fields only a few miles apart may mature at different times. During the late summer, Navajo carry on an active trade in vegetables from fields that have matured and are later repaid in vegetables from fields that have not yet matured. By summer's end, vegetable-starved Navajo undertake long trips to obtain a few ears of corn from the field of a relative.

The techniques of farming are not complex, nor are farming skills of much importance in building personal prestige. The crops provide a small amount of extra food and help stay the family over the hunger-filled winter. After the fresh vegetable period, surplus corn is dried, hung on strings, and later ground on a stone slab into flour that is used as the basis for fried bread and mush. However, the fields of the Nez Ch'ii area are not able to produce anywhere near the amount of food needed for the present population, so increasingly the Navajo have become dependent on food purchased from the trader, principally wheat flour and potatoes.

Despite the fact that agriculture does not play an important role and, compared to livestock husbandry, is decreasing in importance with each generation, one product of agriculture is singularly important to the Navajo. Corn pollen is considered perhaps the most sacred of all the substances of the universe. It is carried as an amulet in small buckskin bags, is used to bless persons, animals, and hogans, and is a part of every Navajo ritual. This reflects the important influence the Pueblo peoples, who also revere corn pollen, have had on Navajo religious and ritual life.

Learning To Farm

The techniques of farming are few and simple. As a matter of course both boys and girls learn how to harness a team for ploughing. Men generally do the ploughing, and one male in the homestead group may in fact plough all the fields for his sisters or sisters-in-law. But he takes no special pride in a straight furrow or the other traditional signs of competence so proudly displayed by White farmers. Beyond the ploughing there is only the placing of the seeds and the unskilled business of hoeing weeds and picking the crop. What little has to be learned is learned casually by children helping their parents.

Today most fields are fenced to keep out livestock, and perhaps fence making, not a very popular art among the free-ranging Navajo, should be included as one of the agricultural skills learned by young men from older men who themselves may have picked up the art from watching or working with White men.

An interesting aspect of Navajo agriculture is the making of scarecrows. Among the nearby Hopis, birds are frightened away by draping lengths of cloth on frames or on the limbs of trees. The Navajo on the other hand are apt to display considerable ingenuity and wit in constructing human figures by using sticks and old clothes. Often family groups—men, women, and children—will be placed in the field in attitudes of work or waving at passersby. They seldom discourage birds but they add an element of whimsy to an otherwise tedious, hot, and not too rewarding activity in an often bleak landscape.

Gathering

Although hunting provides a basis of skills useful in herding, gathering seems little related to farming. In the past, we believe, the Navajo were gatherers as well as hunters. Recent traditions describing the thin days after the return from Fort Sumner describe extensive gathering activities. Today these have all but disappeared. In the spring, herders or children playing may dig up small bulbous root plants and eat them on the spot but never bring them home or gather them in amounts large enough to be considered as part of the family food supply.

Most women know a number of plants used to make native dyes for weaving and, with their daughters in attendance, go on collecting expeditions during the spring and summer. A number of plants used for herbal remedies are also collected, but, aside from this, gathering plays almost no part in Navajo life save in the case of the piñon.

In the northern reaches of the Navajo country the piñon pine, which bears large crops of fat seeds in small easily opened cones, grows in profusion. In the past, collecting piñon nuts for food was done by the Navajo just as it is by most of the tribes of the Great Basin (cf. Downs, *The Two Worlds of the Washo*). However, in Nez Ch'ii there are few such trees, and the piñon is not important. In other parts of the reservation relatively large sums of cash can be made by gathering piñon nuts for sale to traders who then sell them to confectioners. Only rarely does a Navajo from Nez Ch'ii undertake such work.

Farming and the Nuclear Unit

The herds symbolize the unity of the homestead groups and the continuity of the various matrilines. The fields would appear to have important symbolic relation to the nuclear unit.

As noted before, farming is the responsibility of nuclear units rather than the homestead group. As such, it constitutes the basic element of survival for the nuclear unit. A man and wife without relatives are hard pressed to manage more than a few sheep. As a team, however, they and their children can put in and harvest a crop. The most vigorous and industrious farmers are apt to be people unfortunate enough to be separated from their relatives by circumstances of death. Similarly, poverty in the Navajo sense is often symbolized by devotion to one's corn crop as a final desperate attempt to survive through one's own efforts. Hard work is a positive value among the Navajo, and a poor man who works hard in his fields is admired but pitied. In the past, the Navajo who maintained large and prosperous farms in Canyon DeChelle were considered unfortunates because they did not have large herds.

Another occasion on which farming is emphasized is when a large homestead group begins to fragment. This most frequently takes place after a period of disagreement and at least minor quarreling. As the individual nuclear units begin to separate from the original homestead group, they take with them their sheep, each to form the nucleus of a new herd. Usually such herd fragments are very small and not in any sense economical. As each unit reestablishes itself, its members devote themselves wholeheartedly to clearing new fields and planting a new crop. Consciously or not, they seem to respond to the new situation in which for the time being at least, they do not have the cooperative support of the other members of the homestead group interacting around the combined sheep herd. In short, the herding operations of Nez Ch'ii tend to extend and elaborate interpersonal relations, while the farming activities are oriented toward smaller units and fewer relationships.

8

Religion

PERHAPS NO OTHER ASPECT of Navajo life has been so thoroughly studied as has Navajo religious practices and beliefs. The consequence of this emphasis on religion has been the development of a somewhat out-of-focus view of the Navajo. Laymen, in particular, are apt to see the many works on religion and ritual as representing the priorities of Navajo culture and gain an impression of a people totally immersed in the holy and the sacred and somehow isolated from the mundane and profane. Nothing could be further from the truth. The Navajo, being hard-headed and pragmatic, is as able to judge objective reality as the next man and can be just as concerned about material comfort and social status as others are. However, unlike us, his "being religious" does not preclude his acting in an everyday way. In short, the Navajo view of the supernatural does not really make that distinction. The universe is of a single piece; it is all natural, and man is a part of that universe and must adhere to its many laws. The laws, however, are known—if not in detail to every Navajo, in general; he knows how to behave from time to time and situation to situation so that he may keep the universe in order and balance. To put his shoes on the wrong feet, as a very minor example, will bring about his death, not because putting shoes on the wrong feet is a sin but because the order of the world has been for an instant shaken. Old men believe that the lack of rain in recent years is due to the fact that young men are cutting their hair after the fashion of the White man. Long hair encourages rain; it is the natural order of things, and the results are inevitable and understandable. To deny this order is as wrongheaded to a Navajo as it is to argue that the earth is flat in our own world.

The famous anthropologist Bronislaw Malinowski suggested many years ago that primitive magic was a kind of science or ancestor to science. Many people, perhaps most, have not agreed with that view totally, but in a sense the Navajo support this idea. For us, science, with its laws of motion and gravity and its knowledge of germs and microbes, provides a background of explanation for our actions and for the things which happen around us—rain storms, hurricanes, earthquakes, and the like. For the Navajo, his religion is the explanation not only for what happens but for what one must do in order to keep the universe in order.

We, with our nuclear weapons and pollutants, have only recently accepted the notion that we are responsible for destroying ourselves and our environment. The Navajo has for centuries lived with the idea that he, by some careless act, some small failure to observe proper behavior, could upset the balance of the world and create disaster. Thus his religion, if we may call it that, is a matter of constantly observing the laws of the universe rather than the commands of God. He has little real theology but much wisdom that can be applied to everyday life. There are many Navajo ritual practitioners but no body of Navajo priests. Some men speculate and imagine, while others do not, being satisfied merely to carry out the prescriptions of ritual. Thus, following models of religious study formulated in their own history, scientists and scholars of another culture impose the sort of order on Navajo theology that is implied even in this brief section. For instance, those who study the religion in depth have had great difficulty in distinguishing various mythological figures that appear, disappear, and reappear in Navajo mythology. This difficulty troubles us, but it does not seem to bother the Navajo, who are no more concerned with the incongruities of their origin story than the fundamentalist Christian is troubled by incongruities in Genesis.

The Myth

Dine, the Navajo term for themselves, means literally "People of the Surface of the Earth." The origin myth of the Navajo describes the ascent of the ancestors of the People of the Surface of the Earth to the surface and the adventures and miraculous happenings that led to the establishing of traditional Navajo life. It could be considered an allegory describing the wanderings of the Athapaskan-speaking peoples and their eventual arrival in the Southwest. It incorporates elements of mythology that are almost universal in the New World. Some themes even appear to have relations to myth elements common in Asia. Certain aspects of myth and ritual reflect association with other Southwestern people, especially the Hopi and other Pueblo tribes. Still other things are unique to the Navajo or at least to the Southwestern Athapaskans.

Before there were Earth Surface People, there were, and are, the Holy People who once lived in the lowest of twelve worlds below the present surface of the earth. The Holy People are holy because they are powerful—not because they are perfect. It was in each instance some act of mischief or malice that forced the Holy People to move into a higher world. Usually one among them practiced witchcraft against the others and forced the move. In each world there were adventures and events that still have effect on the people of today. Practices were established, knowledge was created, and even special types of people appeared. For instance, in the third or fourth world (there is disagreement in the different versions of the myth) there appeared hermaphrodites or transvestites, men who dress and act like women. Such people today and in the past are somewhat venerated by the Navajo and considered to have potential supernatural power. In the last world but one, men and women quarreled bitterly and decided to live separately, each sex on the opposite side of the river. The men, according to the myth, lived quite harmoniously, learning the skills of women and even inventing some important household implements and techniques. The women, on the other hand, after getting off to a good start, were unable to suppress their sexual urges. Details vary, but it would seem that they engaged in homosexual intercourse and also had intercourse with monsters. From these relations there sprang a whole series of monsters who were to plague the Navajo for a long time—some of them even today. Eventually the sexes reached a rapprochement and rejoined each other to live in traditional harmony. But soon a great flood began to fill the eleventh world, and the Holy People were forced to scramble up through a hollow reed to the surface of the earth.

On the earth, the natural objects were formed, the landscape shaped either by powers of the universe or by the Holy People themselves. Death appeared for the first time.

Prominent among the Holy People were First Man and First Woman, who were created from two ears of corn and who are felt by some to have created the Universe (or at least First Man is given that honor). But their important role is that of mother and father of Changing Woman, the most important figure in Navajo mythology. Her conception and birth were miraculous affairs, but the original pair raised her and trained and allowed her to mate with the Sun and with Water. This mating or matings (it's difficult to know) produced two sons, twins, who grew up to seek out their father the Sun and receive from him weapons and knowledge that allowed them to slay the monsters plaguing the earth and The People. The record of their victories is written in the landscape of the Navajo country. Prominent mountains, lava flows, and other natural features are identified with the carcasses of slain monsters.

The Twin Monster Slayers are considered by some students of the subject to be War Gods, and their lives serve as a model for traditional Navajo male behavior.

Their mother, however, is more properly thought of as a personification of the earth itself, for she is forever growing old and withered only to emerge again, as does the earth in the spring, as a young and beautiful woman.

These figures are certainly not the only ones in Navajo mythology. There are dozens of Holy People, and it is often hard to distinguish one from the other. Is White-Shell-Woman, for instance, a sister of Changing Woman, or is she Changing Woman herself in a different form? Each of these Holy People, or *Yei* as they are called in Navajo, is associated with specific natural features of the land, with other *yei*, and with aspects of the weather, vegetation, mineral deposits, and with certain animals. Perhaps one illustration of these complex relations is needed before we discuss religion as it is acted out in day-to-day life. In her book *Navajo Religion* Alice Riechard describes the relations of a single *yei*, Talking God. His direction is the west; color, yellow; mountain, Mt. Humphreys. He is related to the sunbeam, yellow clouds, and a yellow light in the evening. Among things used as jewels, he is the abalone shell. Among the birds he is symbolized by the yellow warbler, and as vegetation he is black or yellow corn. Other *yei* who live on Mt. Humphreys are

White Corn Boy, Yellow Corn Girl, Evening Light Boy, and Abalone Girl. Dark Clouds, male (?) rain, yellow corn, and wild animals are also associated with this *yei*.

Every Navajo does not know or understand such a systematic approach to the *Yei* who today live at the various points of the compass and at zenith and nadir. However, practitioners are supposed to understand such symbolism so that they will not make errors in rituals. The *Yei* are not in our sense gods, although we often translate the word that way. They can misbehave, make errors, and act with malice. At the same time, they can be controlled and coerced as well as persuaded by proper ritual acts, and it is these acts that form a network of behavioral guideposts for Navajo life. We cannot discuss them in detail but will simply examine some of the more important aspects of ritual and belief.

Daily Activities

It is customary for the eldest male of a Navajo homestead to begin the day at sunrise by singing a sacred song and dropping corn pollen, a singularly sacred substance in all Navajo and Hopi ritual, in the four cardinal directions. Throughout the day that follows, the routine is accompanied by endless and almost unconscious acts of ritual. A sacred song is frequently sung as the sheep herd is taken from the pen for grazing, and snatches of songs often semisacred in nature are heard throughout the day. The manufacture of various tools and utensils is accompanied by often elaborate ritual. The anthropologist Harry Tschopik has suggested that one reason that the Navajo so quickly abandoned native handmade utensils and tools such as baskets, pottery, saddles, and so on is that the ritual involved had become too elaborate and time-consuming, and when alternatives appeared in the form of manufactured goods, they were quickly accepted. Even the flat baskets used as part of the ritual payment to singers and medicine men in virtually all ceremonies are seldom made by the Navajo but instead purchased and repurchased from the local trader who, by long and complex routes, has received them from the Southern Paiute. The making of a bow and arrows is another activity requiring not only technical but also esoteric knowledge. Without the latter, the former would be useless, and the weapon would not perform satisfactorily.

Even such mundane acts as cooking are governed by characters from the mythological past. The simple act of baking a mud-covered prairie dog in the ashes of the cooking fire is explained in the humorous story of Badger and Coyote.

> Badger was hunting prairie dogs and had killed a bunch when he met Coyote. Coyote was hunting, too, but he hadn't caught none of them prairie dogs. He saw all them prairie dogs that Badger had and he tried to figure out how to get them. He said to Badger, "Let's us have a race around that mesa, and the one who wins will get to eat all the prairie dogs." Badger he say, "O.K., but let's put them in the ashes of the fire to cook so they will be ready when we get back." So they built a fire and put the prairie dogs in the ashes with just their tails sticking out, and then they started to race. Well, Coyote was real fast, and pretty soon he was out of sight, and Badger he knew all the time that he

couldn't run faster than Coyote. So when Coyote went behind the mesa, Badger he just run back to the fire and pull them prairie dogs out by their tails and ate them. And then he put just the tails back, sticking out of the ashes, and then he went off and hid. Pretty soon Coyote come around the mesa all tired and panting, and he figured he won the race, and so he ran over to the fire laughing about how he'd tricked Badger and grabbed them tails and pulled them out, but there wasn't nothing but tails, and old Badger he laughed and laughed, and that's why we cook prairie dogs the same way Badger and Coyote cooked them.

This story provides an example of how even the most minor aspects of Navajo daily life are shaped and influenced by references to the Navajo cosmology. Like most other American Indians, the Navajo mythically recall a time when men and animals shared a single society, culture, and language. It is difficult to separate the mythical prototypes of modern animals from the actual animals or to understand clearly in what form the actors in such stories appear.

Throughout their daily life, the Navajo also weave a network of sacred or semisacred songs. From the ritual singing at sunrise and while the sheep are being driven from the pen to the singing in the cornfields and during wood gathering, weaving, or spinning, the Navajo homestead is full of song. Sung softly to one's self or in loud self-confident tones, which are always startling in such a barren, generally silent country, the songs call up blessings or bring down protection on the singer, his herds, his family, or the enterprise in which he or she is involved.

One important combination of the sacred and the mundane is the ritual of the sweat-bath. An integral part of each Navajo homestead is a semisubterranean structure that is perhaps two feet deep, three or four feet above ground, and eight to ten feet wide. It is covered over with earth and entered through a very small door that is closed with blankets. This forms an almost airtight sweat room that can be heated to seemingly unendurable temperatures by placing heated rocks in one corner. Usually once a week, sometimes oftener, the men of a homestead take a sweat-bath. The process is a long one requiring the collection of a large wood supply that is used to heat the sweat-rocks. When the rocks are properly heated, the fire-tender calls his companions, and, using a shovel, places the rocks in the sweat-house. Modern Navajo usually take a washtub filled with water as well as soap with them to the sweat lodge. All adult males are required to tie a string around their prepuce before entering the sweat-lodge. To fail to do this would be a very dangerous act. One of the signs of a boy's acceptance as an adult occurs when his father or uncle instructs him to use a prepuce string before entering the lodge. Such a boy is always looked upon with a great deal of envy by his younger contemporaries. Once the rocks are in place, as many men as the small room will hold crowd into the lodge and call to the fire-tender to cover the door. They then begin a round of songs calling for good health, fine healthy animals, good crops, rain, and wealth. The songs are sung in groups of four, and sweating continues through a complete cycle of four, eight, sixteen or even more, depending on the stamina of the sweaters and the size of their repertoire. When the song cycle is finished, the blankets are pulled away, and the sweaters emerge. They dry themselves by rolling in the dust, while praying softly to themselves, and then rinse off with water. Often two groups take turns, or individuals return for yet another cycle of sweating and singing. The sweat bath serves at one time the functions of cleanliness and worship. It can also, as do all other Navajo rituals, include a curing element. Minor ailments are often taken to the sweat-bath. Certain plants that are said to be good for stomach trouble or headaches are carried into the sweat-lodge. Less frequently, and always after sunset, the women of the homestead go to the sweat-house to use the rocks already heated by the men. This use, however, appears to have much less ritual content. Men must stay well away while the women are sweating, and female laughter can be heard for miles across the steppes.

Other aspects of religion and ritual that occur almost incessantly and casually are such things as a constant attention to omens and small personal ritual invocations for health, success, or rain. Regarding omens, one is always alert to signs of danger, the sounds of certain birds or animals, forgetfully putting one's moccasins on the wrong foot (an omen of death), and so forth. An example of a ritual invocation is picking up a horned toad, rubbing it over one's neck and chest, and freeing it along with a prayer to be carried to the forces of nature requesting good health. Also, rain can be encouraged by shooting a variety of swallow that appear in the Navajo country at dusk. It is considered good luck for a traveler to place a stone or a bit of shell or turquoise on cairns established along trails throughout the Navajo country and to say a prayer. These cairns, standing visible for miles in the flat steppelands, mark well-traveled trails and often are as high as a man on horseback.

A stone trail marker on top of a hill indicates older travel routes. The telephone pole marks the route of the automobile roads.

Sings and Singers

The acts described above constitute the daily, casual aspects of Navajo religion. The core of Navajo religious activities, however, is the person of the *hatli*, or "chanter," and the ceremonies (generally called "sings" in English) over which they preside. All ceremonial activities are based on special prayer songs, and one can make only an arbitrary distinction between sings and the ceremonies that will be discussed in the next section.

The Navajo chanter, frequently called a medicine man, is a person who has, through apprenticing him- or herself to an older person, learned certain sacred prayer songs connected with the origin myth. Song is considered an especially powerful force in Navajo life, and many persons have personal songs or know parts of sacred songs, which they sing for their own benefit. Only a recognized practitioner, however, can sing to effect a cure of another person. Singers do not constitute a separate caste of people. They live normal lives and are involved in herding and farming, although a popular singer may have little time for these activities, owing to the demands for his services.

There are many classifications of sings and chants developed by students of Navajo religion; however, we need only consider them in terms of length, elaborateness, and associated activities. In all cases, the expressed purpose of a sing is to cure. The ailment may be an obvious physical complaint or a vague feeling of uneasiness, or it may be overindulgence in drink, gambling, horse racing, marital infidelities, or laziness. There are many dozens of chants and songs and accompanying rituals, and one must know the proper one to use. For this purpose, a diagnostician is called. The singer is a skilled workman who has learned a song and its associated ritual. The diagnostician is a person with certain special talents for divining the basis of the complaint. Some diviners, as they are often called, can handle such mundane matters as finding lost articles and animals. Others have the power to understand what is the cause of a patient's complaint and recommend the proper song, ritual, or chant to effect the cure. Some diviners even specialize in getting to the bottom of domestic problems such as quarreling between members of an outfit.

Once a special song-ritual has been recommended, the patient and his family must send an intermediary to seek out a singer who knows the song, has the ritual paraphernalia, and who is willing to work for them. Sings vary from one-day to five-day affairs. Some may be performed only in a hogan of traditional design. Others can be performed even in the houses of White men. For others it might be necessary to remove the door from a log cabin or White-style house (called *kin* in contrast to the *hogan* or traditional-style dwelling). Still others may require that a special structure, in which the ritual can be performed, be built of brush. The shorter the sing, the fewer are the people involved. A one-night sing—actually taking place in two parts, one in the daytime and the other late at night until dawn—is attended only by the relatives residing in the homestead. But often in such cases it is not considered effective unless all the residents are present at certain parts of the ritual. In almost every instance, a sand painting or design of colored sands, earths, and pollens is made as the beginning step of the ritual, which ends hours later after a night of continuous singing and intermittent ritual directed at the patient. The effectiveness of the performance is based on the skill of the singer, who must know the proper songs in word-for-word perfection, as well as the ritual acts.

Such semiprivate family affairs may last from one to five days, and the larger and larger groups of relatives who often attend the longer sings are asked to share some of the expense of paying the singer. Certain traditional payments are made, such as ears of corn and a flat basket and frequently a tanned deerskin, but, in addition, food stuffs, blankets, sheep, and money are also required.

A singularly important family sing which reflects both the strong matriarchal orientation of Navajo culture and the relationship between Navajo and other Western American tribes is the Girls' Sing. This four-day ceremony is held to announce and celebrate a girl's first menstrual period. The Navajo believe that, during the period of her transition, a girl is particularly sensitive to influences that will affect her later life. She is, in fact, seen as an almost plastic being who can be easily injured and at the same time easily shaped into a proper mold. For four days, then, she remains quiet within her hogan and ventures out during the day only in the earliest dawn to collect wood, run, and act out other virtues of womanhood that reflect hardiness, energy, and a will to work. During each of the four nights she is the center of continuous ceremonial singing by her relatives and friends. The more guests who attend and the more vigorous their singing the more assured is the girl's future. Meanwhile the girl's mother or maternal relatives prepare a large cake of ground corn meal, flavored with sugar and dried fruits and baked in an earth oven. On the morning of the last day, the young woman emerges from her seclusion, and the cake is distributed to all the visitors who come through the faint dawn to congratulate her and her family with their presence.

Public Ceremonies

In contrast to the essentially private, family-oriented sings, there are a number of public ceremonies that include entire communities, in fact, the entire Navajo people. They are, however, not in any sense communal ceremonies. At the base is the same rationale as for the simplest of sings, the need of a person to find a cure for a physical, psychological, or spiritual complaint. In essence there is no difference, save in complexity, between the sings and chants discussed above and the larger ceremonies. The primary emphasis is one of curing, and any ceremony must have one or more patients as a focus of the ritual. However, two types of ceremonies have accumulated a superstructure of social activities, which make of them something far different than a simple curing sing. There are two classes of these ceremonies, depending on when they are performed. The actual chants and rituals performed during the ceremony may differ according to the diagnosis and the skills of the chanter employed.

The squaw dance

Perhaps the most famous and most frequent of these ceremonies is the so-called Squaw Dance, which refers to the social, not the religious, aspects of the occasion. This can be performed only during the warm months, usually after April, although occasionally Squaw Dances have been held as early as March. Originally the Squaw Dance centered on ritual aimed at removing evil influences from the persons of warriors returning from a raid. The association with foreigners, the exposure to death, and the ultimate danger of actually having killed, placed a returning fighter in an extremely dangerous position. Such a purification required four days and nights of ritual overseen by a medicine man familiar with complex chants, sand paintings, and other rituals. To be properly effective, it requires the participation of as many people as possible to lend their assistance to the medicine man and to increase the strength of the ritual through their presence and singing. Paying the chanter and his assistants and feeding the assembled visitors then becomes an undertaking too expensive to be supported by a single homestead group. To meet these expenses the hosts—that is, the family of the patient—call on the most distant of relatives in the matrilineal group as well as groups related through marriage. Guests are also expected to make contributions of food or money, although this is not required and hospitality is extended to anyone who appears. A Squaw Dance given by a rich person or by a family with many connections then may entertain several hundred and sometimes more than a thousand guests. Although the ritual is overtly directed at individual patients, the entire ceremony takes on a communal aspect inasmuch as it requires the cooperation of many people in its planning and execution. Moreover, it also has a spatial dimension, as the ceremonies and attendant social activities take place at three different locations during the course of the four days.

The decision to have such a ceremony rests originally with a single individual who feels ill or suspects that a ritual cure might relieve him of a feeling of despondency or depression, stop his excessive drinking, solve domestic problems, or simply improve his luck. A consultation with the diagnostician confirms his need for a dance, and discussions with the members of the homestead group explore the economics and logistics of such an occasion. Often a poorer family must delay the event until money can be saved and relatives convinced of the necessity of the ritual.

Once the decision is firm, the homestead group of the patient begins making arrangements with nearby consanguinal relatives. A series of meetings are held and arrangements made as to where the three different locations will be; the secondary hosts are requested to cooperate, and arrangements are made to pay them, usually in livestock, for their trouble. Because the original ritual site and the secondary site require the building of elaborate structures and preparing food for large crowds, the second-night host is usually an affinal relative of the patient. In this way, members of the patient's clan are required to assist in the construction of one site, while the members of an affinal clan are involved in the other. Another factor in the planning is the availability of a chanter or medicine man who knows the recommended ritual. There are many rituals suitable for the Squaw Dance, but not all medicine men know them all. Many remain only memories and are no longer practiced because no one remembers the proper procedures.

The actual ceremony itself begins at the site selected by the host, where a special brush hogan is constructed for the medicine man and his assistants and where, more or less continuously, various phases of the ceremony are performed over the four-day period. In addition, wood for cooking and lighting is collected in large amounts, barrels of water assembled, and a large brush ramada, where the women of the host clan prepare food, is constructed. Sheep and cattle are collected from relatives and held ready for slaughtering as needed. Quantities of flour, coffee, and other foods are purchased from the trader and delivered to the hosts.

The activities for which the ceremony is popularly named has nothing to do with the ritual being performed and is entirely social. The returning of warriors in the past was seen as a good time to announce the readiness of young women for marriage. These young unmarried women, dressed in their best clothing and displaying their wealth in turquoise and silver, appeared each night to select partners to join them in a simple shuffling dance. The primacy of women in Navajo life

Almost merging with its background, a brush hogan stands abandoned after a Squaw Dance. The ceremonial aspects of the event take place largely in this kind of structure.

is again reflected in the etiquette of the dance. No young man, once selected, can refuse to dance with a girl unless he can prove that he is a member of the girl's or some other ineligible clan. Should a man refuse, the girl's mother, aunts, and older sisters may well descend upon him and drag him into the center of the circle of wagons and campfires that forms each night. If a young man does not want to carry the affair further, he must make some small payment at the end of the dance. Should he refuse to pay, he binds the young woman to be his partner through the rest of the dance. If she has second thoughts about her choice, she is trapped unless she can steal his hat, blanket, or some other possession and ransom it, thus receiving the payment necessary to free her.

In addition to the courtship dance, which is the focal point of a great deal of good-natured ribaldry and not a little jealousy because girls can select married as well as unmarried men, there are round dances performed by both men and women, married and unmarried, and team singing. The singing teams form quite casually and are made up of men of all ages, who, while swaying back and forth, sing traditional and often spontaneously composed "Squaw Dance songs," accompanied by a small pottery drum. This gives rise to the term *swaying songs* often used to describe these compositions. Navajo vocal music is particularly distinctive because it is performed with great throat tension and with an emphasis on high-pitched

One of the principles in the Squaw Dance mounting his horse to lead the procession to the site of the second night of ceremonial singing and dancing. The decorated cedar branch is the focus of the four-day ceremony.

nasal sounds. The newcomer who is not familiar with Navajo music generally assumes that women are singing until he sees the crowds of young men.

In the days between the night dances, while rituals are being conducted by the medicine man, the visiting families camp near their wagons, visit relatives and friends, gamble, stage horseraces, and continue diffidently the courtships that began the night before.

On the final day, the arrival of young warriors is reenacted and presents of bread, cakes, candy, and fruit are thrown to the crowd. If the host can afford it, the events of the day may also be enlivened by young men who, disguised with simple masks and daubed with mud, act as clowns and terrorize the crowd by seizing hapless individuals and dumping them in the mud or otherwise harrassing them. The clowns also confer some benefits of health by seizing a person and, while chanting, carrying him on a blanket. Persons suffering minor or chronic ailments or those seeking a change in luck volunteer for the treatment.

Although the orientation of the Squaw Dance is familial and individual in practice, it involves all, or at least a large part, of the community, by defining relationships, establishing obligations, and providing the opportunity to pay off old ones. It is an occasion of social display—wearing one's best clothing and jewelry, displaying one's horses and wagons (and in later years trucks and autos), initiating courtship, and engaging in illicit liaison. Failure to take part in a family's Squaw Dance is tantamount to admitting a serious breach within the structure of the family. At the same time, a well-known or powerful family entertains visitors who "drop in" from throughout the reservation as a symbol of friendship and support. Relatives absent from the community are informed and expected to return home to take part, even, and this is often the case, if it means giving up off-reservation employment. At the same time, the collection of livestock and other food stuffs, the presenting of gifts to the host, the payment of the chanter and his assistants, the feeding of participants and guests, the exchanging of money and goods in gambling, and the purchase of supplies from the trader mean that each Squaw Dance has an enormous impact on the economic life of the community.

The flexibility within prescribed patterns that characterizes Navajo social structure can also be seen in ceremonial life. Since the defeat of the Navajo, the military aspect of Navajo culture has gradually disappeared. However, the ceremonies surrounding the warrior's life were extended to serve as protection for anyone exposed to foreigners—children returning from school, women working as domestics off-reservation, traders, Bureau of Indian Affairs officers, or anyone else suffering from what might be diagnosed as dangerous contact with foreigners. After World War II, returning veterans almost without exception were the focal point of a Squaw Dance to ward off the evil influences of their wartime experiences.

In the past, the Squaw Dance ceremonies appear to have been held less frequently than in recent years, perhaps only a few each summer on the entire reservation. In modern times, especially since World War II, hundreds of such ceremonies are held each summer throughout the reservation area. This may be a result of the greater felt need as a result of increasing contact with outsiders. On the other hand, the gradually deteriorating economic conditions on the reservation may be the basis for more frequent attempts to correct whatever supernatural evil has befallen individual families. There is also a distinct element of competition in the staging of Squaw Dances in any given area. The occurrence of one dance almost always is followed by another and yet another, until it would seem that the psychic and economic energy of a community is exhausted. In part, this is the consequence of each homestead group's wishing to display its status by staging the most impressive dance possible. In part, too, the decision to hold a dance may be motivated by the knowledge that as more and more dances are held the ability of relatives and friends to contribute is reduced, so each family considering the possibility of a dance speeds up its decision. In the Nez Ch'ii area in the summer of 1960, thirteen such events occurred within a radius of about twenty miles. The summer before, only two dances were held, as a response to real physical illnesses, and in the following year only four dances were held. A dance cycle such as the one in 1960 is particularly exhausting physically and economically to persons of influence and political aspirations and those who have many lines of kinship in a given area. One such man, the chairman of the local grazing committee, felt obliged to appear at every dance, to make speeches and participate in the ceremonies for which he always received a gift of tanned buckskin, food, or a plush shirt; ruefully contemplating yet another dance, he said, "I hope them people don't give me no nice presents. I can't afford no more presents." His problem was that the giving of presents anticipated a reciprocal act that he could no longer afford. Yet, to maintain his position in the community, he felt required to repay each gift even if it meant going into debt at the trading post.

Yeibeichai DANCES

The mobile nature of the summer Squaw Dance reflects perhaps the mobility of Navajo life in the summer as well as the network of relationships within which each homestead group rests. The winter ceremonies on · the other hand are not mobile and for a number of reasons are less frequently performed. Again, a great number of separate chants and rituals can be performed in the winter, but the general class of ceremonies at which they occur are called the *Yeibeichai* dances. The fact that the *Yei* are represented by masked men and can appear only in the winter months suggests that they may, in part, at least, represent religious figures borrowed from the neighboring Pueblo peoples, with their colorful cycle of *Kachina* dances. In any event, a *Yeibeichai* dance is even more expensive and complex than the Squaw Dance, inasmuch as nine days and nights of ritual are required in order to complete it. Because chanters who know the entire complex ritual of a nine-day ceremony are rarer than Squaw Dance medicine men, because the feeding of large numbers of people for nine nights is exceedingly expensive, and because travel is more difficult in the winter, thus preventing the kind of enjoyable socializing associated with the Squaw Dance, the *Yeibeichai* dances are not as frequently performed. However, in the event of some disaster or illness which cannot be otherwise treated, there is no alternative. The dances, with costumed dancers or the social Fire Dance in which fire brands are whirled and thrown into the darkness, are more spectacular than the night performances at a Squaw Dance, and in a sense the rituals associated with the *Yeibeichai* are considered more powerful simply because they are more complex. Some of these chants are associated with the bear, and the dances are never held before the traditional time when the bear goes into hibernation. In the past, particularly ambitious medicine men have attempted to use live bears or bear cubs in the ceremonies, but the results have often been disastrous and dangerous, so that the animal, particularly fearsome and sacred to the Navajo, is represented only in symbol.

Of the actual rituals performed in either the Squaw Dance or the *Yeibeichai* dances we will probably never have a complete accounting. Some of them, associated with activities no longer important to the Navajo, such as antelope hunting, remain memories but are no longer practiced. Others have fallen into disuse because the medicine men who knew the correct chants and rituals have died without passing on their knowledge.

The rituals, skills, paraphernalia, and songs necessary to conduct such a ceremony are exceedingly complex and require years to memorize under the tutelage of a practicing medicine man. This must be paid for with personal service or wealth in livestock, food, or money. Learned in any other way, without payment, the knowledge would be of no value because it would, in effect, be stolen and thus not the true property of the practitioner.

Among the neighboring Hopi, the rituals and ceremonies follow a pre-destined pattern through the year in a cycle of dances that mark different phases of the year and assure in each ceremonial step that the rains will fall at the right time and the crops will come to fruition when they are expected. The role of each man and woman is determined in relationship to the community, his clan, or cult membership; the ceremony is not the function of a family but of the entire community.

The Navajo ceremonial complex is equally as symbolic of the structure of his society as is that of the Hopi, and it reflects the flexible nature of Navajo life and the importance of the homestead group on which each Navajo, in the final analysis, must depend for survival. Thus, while each Hopi plays a predetermined role in each ceremony according to his status in the community, the Navajo participates in terms of his relationships to the host family. If his homestead is the sponsor, his duties and responsibilities are many and often onerous. If, on the other hand, the sponsor is a distant relative or a friend, the individual Navajo may or may not be expected to contribute and participate heavily. Thus, while a person might take part in as many as a dozen ceremonies in a single year, each ceremony will present itself from a different perspective and emphasize the person's relationship, not to the community as a whole, but rather to each homestead unit that makes up the community. Only an understanding of all the complex interrelations provides a definition of community.

Death and the Dead

The people of Nez Ch'ii, like most other Navajo, do not fear death any more or less than do other people. However, like many Western Indians, notably those of the Great Basin, they do fear the dead. The dead are dangerous because the ghost of a dead man may return to trouble the living. There are no good ghosts in Navajo life. A ghost is the evil part of a total man. It may return because its property has been mishandled or expropriated or because of ritual failures. It is possible for a ghost to harm the living by entering their bodies. Thus it is best to avoid the dead, lest one is exposed to such a visitation. There is great danger in being near the dead, whether they are former friends or former enemies. To escape the danger that such association raises one must undergo long and expensive ritual treatment.

Thus, when a person has died in a hogan, for instance, the structure is abandoned. The body is often left inside with its belongings. Burial is rapid and without much ceremony, and, in the past at least, a person's favorite valuable possessions were buried with them. Early traders and missionaries were often tolerated by the Navajo because they would volunteer to bury the dead, thus freeing the Navajo from the fearsome task. Similarly, hospitals were used as a place where one could take an obviously dying sick person so that the hogan did not have to be abandoned; this was perhaps also done to confuse the ghost so it could not return to plague the living. The consciousness of the presence and danger of ghosts is expressed in fear of the dark and a reluctance to go out at night, as well as in avoidance of funerals and of obviously dying people.

Witches, Werewolves, and Society

The power of Navajo songs, chants, prayers, and ritual is compulsive. A prayer is not a supplication but the activation of natural forces, the outcome of which is a foregone conclusion. An error in manipulating these forces, a mistaken word in a chant, an error in the preparation of a sand painting, or the omission of some act renders the ritual ineffective and sometimes can be quite dangerous for the patient, the practitioner, and the community. Errors of course can be set right, but if an error in ritual can be dangerous, what of deliberate error? Navajo logic holds that chants sung backwards or ritual deliberately performed improperly can bring disaster to the community or to individuals. They further believe that just as there are good medicine men who have labored and paid to learn blessing chants, there are others who have labored and paid even more to learn evil chants. These witches, both male and female, can bring illness and disaster on enemies, and their influence is constantly feared. It is a fear of coming under the spell of a witch that makes Navajo careful and wary in large crowds. Seldom does a person go to even purely Navajo affairs without the support of familiar company, preferably relatives or close friends. Nor does a Navajo relish staying alone, particularly at night. One seldom sees women alone, even in the daytime, and although men may travel alone in the daylight, they try to find company before nightfall. Particularly when going to a large gathering, a Navajo wears charms and amulets, often simple bags of sacred corn pollen, to protect himself from danger.

NEGATION OF NAVAJO ETHIC

Despite the strong belief in witches and witchcraft and extensive study by anthropologists, witchcraft is an elusive subject. Almost anyone who has gained the confidence of Navajo people has heard endless stories of witches and "wolf men" and heard vague accusations against one or another person, usually a non-relative living at some distance from the accuser. In addition, he has been told how the death of one or another person close to the teller has been traced to the evil influences of a witch. Navajo can describe in detail the initiation of witches to a coven, the murder of relatives, and incest and nakedness in mixed groups. All of these are violations of the most important strictures of Navajo morality. Murder brings down danger on the murderer and the community as a whole. Incest, of course, is a singularly dangerous act abhorred by even the most depraved. And while the Navajo are relatively casual among themselves about nudity above the waist, exposure of the genitals by even the youngest of children, particularly girls, is a serious breach of etiquette. In short, the witch presents a reverse picture of what a good Navajo should be and a negative emphasis of the Navajo ethic. Whether or not there are people who actually undergo the initiation of witches and believe they can perform evil deeds through evil chants and ritual is a matter of conjecture. The individual Navajo believes that such people exist, and he governs his behavior accordingly. A person suspected of witchcraft, particularly if he or she is suspected of directing his power against one's person or relatives, may, if all other means fail, be killed in self-defense. Such killings, officially unexplained by White law, still occur. A less drastic cure is to seek the aid of a chanter who knows the proper rituals to counteract evil spells. Although seldom declared outright, this is often a reason for holding a Squaw Dance or *Yeibeichai* ceremony.

THE WOLF MAN

The most frightening figure among Navajo witches is the "wolf man." Such a person is felt to be able to transform himself into a wolf or coyote and, while in this form, bewitch his enemies by sprinkling a magic substance containing ground parts of human infants through the smoke hole of a hogan. Few Navajo attain adult status without having some experience that they interpret as having to do with wolf men. A man riding alone at dusk and spotting a stray dog near the trail will spur his horse into a gallop and ride into the homestead wide-eyed and breathless, convinced that the animal was a wolf man. Any unusual sound in the night is explained as being made by the wolf man. A sudden paroxysm of barking by the homestead's dogs is considered a sure sign that a wolf man is prowling in the darkness. If it persists, the men of the homestead arm themselves with all the weapons the family can muster and fearfully probe into the darkness. A wolf man can be killed by ordinary bullets, and many stories circulate about the tracks of a wounded coyote suddenly changing into the tracks of a wounded man. Killing a wolf man is a dangerous event because the killer will most certainly be the object of vengeance on the part of the wolf man's relatives, who in all probability are themselves witches.

Jimmie Yazzie, he was married to my sister. He was a good man and worked hard and took care of his kids. In the winter he was hunting—looking in the snow for tracks. It was getting pretty dark, and then he saw this coyote or wolf or dog, and it was real close and he shot it. He knew he hit it, but all of a sudden it was gone. So he went home, and the next day he went back to where he had shot that thing, and he found the tracks and blood, and they went to a place under a tree, but they never went away from the tree. The trail away from the tree was a girl's tracks, and they went over to the west toward where an old man and woman lived with their granddaughter. And we heard that she came home one night, and she had been shot and died the next day. So we knew what it was. And that Jimmie Yazzie, he died six months later.

FEAR AS CULTURAL REINFORCEMENT

The complex of mythology, omens, and ritual that make up the "good" aspects of Navajo religion all function to reinforce the structures and attitudes essential to the survival of Navajo society. Stressing the "evil" aspects is no less important in confirming the proper behavior in the Navajo individual.

Many observers have noted that Navajo child training, in keeping with general Navajo interpersonal relationships, is generally lacking in coercive practices. That is, whipping and other corporal punishment to enforce proper behavior does not occur as frequently as it might in a non-Navajo family. However, Navajo make skillful use of terror to instill in their children, and reinforce in adults, the most important attitude in Navajo life—dependence on the immediate relatives of the homestead group. As mentioned earlier, the Navajo seldom travel alone, always preferring to be in groups and preferably groups of relatives. The most innocent departure from this norm is met with great emotion. Members of a family are constantly worried lest some other member "run away" from the family. Even a casual walk by oneself is considered a suspect act. In fact, a desire to be alone and to go for lonely walks is evidence to the individual and to his or her family that something serious is the matter, probably the evil influence of a witch.

To instill this dependence on the group, the Navajo not only encourage loyalty to the family through positive admonition, but also through fear. From infancy, children are exposed to frightening experiences from which they can be extricated only by their mothers or older sisters. A common practice for older children is to dress up in old clothes, often using a coyote or wildcat pelt, and to paint their faces with charcoal and other pigments and appear suddenly to terrorize infants and very young children. The frightened youngsters flee to the arms of their mothers, who usually let them continue their frightened outbursts for several minutes and often add to the fright by pretending fear on their own part. Only when the infant is nearly hysterical with fear does the mother cover its eyes and comfort it and protect it from the horrible monster. Such experiences can only suggest to the infant mind that safety exists solely in relation to mother. The costumed monster may be related to the similar but much more complex institution among the Hopis. The use of fear to instill family adherence is also practiced through the telling of stories about wolf men, witches, and other fearsome beings. Again, as with so many Navajo institutions, there is little formality in the behavior involved. Only after repeated exposures is it possible to realize that what seems like a casual childish prank is a regular activity and is intimately linked to the structure of the society as a whole. Almost every evening, the older children, from eight through twelve years of age, begin to tell stories about evil beings to the younger toddlers and soon have them in a state of abject fear. During this performance, older children and parents watch and listen with much amusement and only in the final extreme of infantile terror offer protecting arms and comforting words. But the cycle does not stop with infants. The teen-age children and adults join in the recounting of tales of witches and wolf men and soon reduce the eight- to twelve-year-olds to states of terror as abject as that of the infants they were previously tormenting. In the telling, the older children and adults usually manage to frighten themselves, and by full dark entire families, fearful of the unknown dangers of the dark and feeling safe only in the protection of their family are crouched in their hogans. Thus, the network of beliefs works from infancy to adulthood to reinforce the idea that only with one's close relatives can one feel safe and only to them can one turn for comfort, aid, and protection. In short, the homestead group is emphasized and reemphasized as the single refuge in an otherwise hostile world. Its needs transcend all others, and its loyalties are more lasting and dependable than all others.

9

Wealth and the Traders

DESPITE THE SCHOOL BUILDINGS, the missionary chapels, the glaring white medical station, and the chapter house, the dominant structure in Nez Ch'ii is the Nez Ch'ii Mercantile Company. In an area where buildings, both native and foreign, tend to be built low, the trading post stands ten feet above the hard packed earth that forms a "town square." Built of native fieldstone in 1918, the trading post has grown over the years to include a cluster of cabins and modern house trailers, a building in which the diesel electric generator rumbles and pops, a wool shed, a service station and garage, the local post office, a small restaurant, and a tangle of holding pens and corrals. A well-shaded wooden porch, fitted with benches, stretches across the front, where double doors open into a gloomy interior.

Although the federal government and the Navajo tribal government and missionaries have had their impact on Nez Ch'ii, their presence is a foreign and dissident element in the community. The trading post, however, stands as an accepted, almost indigenous, institution essential to Nez Ch'ii life. Without the trading post, Navajo culture could never have developed as it has. The role of the trader is as real and as important to Navajo life as is that of the shepherd or the medicine man, and yet the trader is not a Navajo. He is, as are most traders on the reservation, a member of a family that has roots three and more generations deep in the reservation and in Navajo society and that has developed the institution that links Navajo life with the rest of the world.

Status Symbolism

In the popular mind, tribal people are unencumbered by considerations of wealth and status symbolism that so plague the modern American or European. Unfortunately, such an idyllic picture seldom, if ever, exists in reality. It is true that some societies have made adaptations to their environment in such a way that technical and material considerations are minor. In many cases, their level of existence is too low to support competition for food and instead emphasizes sharing. But in almost every case competition for prestige, for control over the activities of other men, is symbolized by a struggle for something. Often the symbols of wealth or importance are not recognized by people unfamiliar with the patterns of foreign cultures. In some cases it may be as ephemeral as supernatural power, acquired fortuitously from the spirit world. Perhaps finely chiseled but totally nonutilitarian blades of obsidian, ornamental plates of copper, the scalps of woodpeckers, elaborate tattooing, or a large number of wives are the goals for which various tribal peoples contend. To a money-oriented modern man such things seem unimportant. The Navajo, however, recognize as wealth much of what their White fellow citizens also consider important. They strive to acquire things that make life easier, more comfortable, or more secure, or that are important enough to influence in their own favor the actions of other men in return for some of these goods. Nonetheless, Navajo economic life has always been one in which men expended efforts in order to secure the necessities rather than amass capital. Many Navajo attitudes about sharing and accumulation of wealth tend to restrict unrestrained accumulation by individuals.

Pressures to share one's good fortune with relatives and a fear of being accused of acquiring wealth by means of witchcraft both restrain the acquisitive impulse, although they most certainly do not suppress it altogether.

For well over a century, the Navajo have been acquainted with and able to handle money. Their own language uses the Spanish term *peso* (Navajo, *beso*) to mean money, and the Navajo counting system reflects experience with various currencies. However, money is not the basis of the traditional Navajo concept of wealth. Money serves only to buy real wealth, that is, "goods."

There are two kinds of "goods" considered to be wealth by the Navajo— hard and soft. Hard goods include silver and turquoise jewelry, saddles, silver horse gear, wagons, and other durable materials. Soft goods include blankets, good clothing —especially plush shirtwaists and satin skirts—tanned buckskins, special flat hand-woven baskets of traditional design, hats, and other less durable items. In describing a person's wealth, a Navajo speaks with awe of a man who owns "eight hats he don't never wear," as well as the number of spare saddles, mule collars, wagons, and shirts he possesses.

The basis of all wealth, however, is livestock. Not only is it possible to trade livestock for any other valuable object or to sell it and obtain money to buy wealth, but animals in and of themselves are wealth and visible symbols of wealth. Traditionally, the Navajo made little distinction in value between individual animals, particularly sheep. Older Navajo speak a bit resentfully of what they consider the unfair, new, and somewhat demeaning practice of weighing individual animals and paying for them by weight. They much prefer a flat "per head" price, even though it might result in a monetary loss overall.

In the past, most certainly the difference in worth between an old and de-crepit horse and a fast racer was recognized and the price set accordingly, but nonetheless a horse, any horse, was wealth and a living symbol of its owner's prosperity and importance. Because of this attitude, the Navajo tended to collect great herds of horses, often composed largely of undesirable and unusable animals, but the owning of such a herd conferred too much prestige to ever permit culling it. Similar attitudes toward the mere size of sheep and cattle herds affected the quality of Navajo livestock. This attitude, of course, worked to the disadvantage of the Navajo when articulating with the economy of the rest of the world. Ill-bred sheep had poor wool, which they often shed in large amounts before shearing time. Moreover, it grew in various colors and required laborious separating, thus lowering the price received for wool. The hardy, shaggy near-wild "Navajo" sheep brought virtually no price in the livestock markets, and, consequently, today many livestock contracts in the Southwest contain a clause guaranteeing that no "Navajo" sheep are present in a lot offered for sale. Similarly, Navajo horses, often undersized and useful only to a man who had dozens of animals from which to draw, had almost no value to outside traders except as dog food.

Establishment of the Trader

As low as the price might be, Navajo wool did have a value, as did Navajo rugs, sheep pelts, cattle hides, and jewelry. To make a profit on these items the traders began to appear in the Navajo country even before the time of military defeat and incarceration.

These earliest traders were enterprising Mormons pushing into the northern Navajo country from the expanding Mormon settlements in Utah. After the Navajo returned from incarceration, the Mormons began to establish more permanent posts in the northern and western areas of the reservation. In the east, where many Navajo had been forced to depend on government rations during the early years of their return, another type of trader developed. The disbursement of rations was generally in the hands of civilian contractors attached to the army as sutlers.* Always alert to a profit, these men began exchanging surplus rations for whatever wool, hides, or other valuable goods the Navajo might have. Soon, as the Navajo economy became more and more vigorous, the sutlers left the army to establish posts throughout the eastern and central portions of the reservation. Nearly one-half of the over two hundred posts now operating in or near the reservation are operated by the descendents of perhaps a dozen families, Mormon or gentile, that pioneered the trading business among the Navajo.

In order to make a profit, the trader has developed a unique business. He learned quickly that if he was to trade with the independent and haughty Navajo, he must adapt himself to the practices of his customers. A kind of pidgin Navajo called "trader" Navajo was developed to enable the Indian and the White man to do business. He found that he must provide any number of services for his customers for which he received no recompense. The distasteful and dangerous job of burying the dead was often left to the trader. Perhaps a rampaging, sheep-killing bear threatened the herds. More often than not, the trader would be informed, and his customers would then retire and wait for him to kill the animal and thus incur the dangerous wrath of the Bear Spirit. Or perhaps the trader would be called

---

* Those who provide provisions for an army post; often established in a shop on the post.

upon to represent the local Navajo before the government agent or in court. In later years the trader assumed the role of hiring agent for the railroads as they sought Navajo workers. As such, he also supervised unemployment, injury, and pension claims. In recent years he has begun filling out the income tax returns of those of his customers whose earnings are high enough.

From the trader the Navajo was able to obtain the material goods of the outside world without becoming personally exposed himself to the dangerous presence of foreigners on his homeground. A taste for coffee had been acquired at Fort Sumner, along with a need for sugar. Commercial ground flour was both easier to use than the hand-ground corn flour and available at the trader's when the supply of corn ran out. Manufactured saddles, bridles, harnesses, wagons, ploughs, and yard goods from which to make the new styles of clothing—all served to attract the Navajo to the trader. As the years have passed, more and more items of White material culture, from kerosene lamps to sewing machines, have become irreplaceable to the Navajo and have formed a material foundation for Navajo culture. The Navajo were able to supply the trader with a number of profit-making commodities in exchange, almost all of which were produced by the herds.

WOOL

Wool is clipped in the spring. Even before the snow has melted, the needs of the individual owner may force him to begin shearing. At this time the activity is carried out by the nuclear family of the owner. Later in the spring the entire homestead group cooperates in shearing the bulk of the herd. The wool of individual owners is sold separately in order that their accounts at the trader's may be kept properly. The sale of wool is the first opportunity the Navajo have to earn money each year, and much of the price is used up immediately in settling credit accounts that have built up during the winter.

LAMBS

In the late summer or early fall, the lambs that were dropped in the spring have matured to market weight and are sold to the trader. The trader holds the lambs in his own corrals until large enough numbers have accumulated to sell them to commission agents. In the recent past the combined herd was driven overland to the railhead, but today livestock trucks haul the animals away. Cash and credit from lamb sales provide an economic buffer against the winter. At this time the trader tries to get all credit accounts brought up to date because there will be little income in the Nez Ch'ii area until the following spring.

HIDES

Much of the actual value of the sheep herd must be reckoned in terms of the contribution that it makes to the family food supply. Sheep are killed for home consumption throughout the year. As the hides accumulate, they are taken to the trader and sold as wool pelts. When a large enough number are collected, the trader in turn sells them to agents who eventually resell them to specialized wool-pulling companies that strip them of wool.

RUGS

In most families, some of the spring wool clip is withheld for use in making rugs. The Navajo rug is a distinctive and well-known item, considered part of the ancient tradition of the Navajo. In fact the Navajo were not weavers until they came into contact with the Pueblo peoples who wove cotton cloth. The Navajo adapted their new skill to wool and for the most part turned the job of weaving, which was a male occupation in the Pueblo villages, over to the women. From their own wool they began to weave rough, long-wearing blankets that served as clothing, especially for women, and robes. Old-fashioned Navajo blankets of this sort were known throughout the West. They were, along with buckskins, the principal item of trade between the Navajo and the Pueblo. Until the 1860s, expeditions of Navajo loaded with blankets were a regular feature of the trading year. Apparently, extensive trade was carried on with the Plains tribes with whom blankets were exchanged for buffalo hides, some of which are still prized heirlooms and used for saddle blankets.

The Navajo rug of today, woven in elaborate designs, is very different from early-day blankets. In the 1890s, traders attempting to develop more profit-making products among the Navajo encouraged the weaving of rugs and the use of both traditional and manufactured dyes. In response to the high prices offered, the Navajo quickly abandoned the older blankets and developed an enormously productive rug-weaving industry.

In Nez Ch'ii almost all adult women are weavers, and the rug trade is an important element in the economic life of the area. The standard rug sizes are single and double saddle blankets, that are either approximately 30 × 30 inches or 30 × 60 inches. Larger sizes are regularly woven by the more expert or ambitious weavers. Rugs measuring up to eighteen to twenty feet are occasionally offered. Such an enterprise often requires the work of two or more women and takes more than a year to complete. When contemplating such a rug, the weaver first consults the trader. If her reputation at her craft is good, he arranges to subsidize the work until the rug is brought in, its value being weighed against trade goods advanced and the difference paid in cash or kind. Such rugs often cost the trader from one to two thousand dollars in trade goods and sell on the outside for upwards of four thousand dollars. Although most weaving is done in the summer when the weather is mild enough to allow the weaver to work outside, rugs are produced throughout the year. A homestead group boasting a few able and energetic weavers is fortunate in having a source of regular although not very high income. A saddle blanket can be finished in a day, but larger rugs require weeks or months, so the hourly income of a weaver is not at all high. Girls learn weaving in the same informal manner in which other skills are taught, by watching their mothers and aunts and older sisters. They may be taught to card wool when still toddlers, be instructed in spinning before they are ten, and begin experimenting on small looms well before they reach puberty. When their work is judged adequate, it is taken to the trader. No matter how uneven and badly made the rug may be, he is wise to make an offer and thus not offend a supplier.

The Navajo themselves use only the smaller rugs as saddle blankets. Large rugs and the bulk of the saddle blankets are made entirely for sale and are never used by the Navajo themselves. The Navajo rug is almost a symbol of the relationship between the people and the trader. Distinctly Navajo in style and technique, it is a product of the combining of the traditions and needs of the Navajo and the Americans, and its utility to the Navajo depends on the trader's acting as agent of its sale. Ironically, when a Navajo wants a soft, colorful "Indian Blanket" to wear, he purchases one made in a factory and sold at the trader's.

JEWELRY

The Spanish and Mexicans taught the Indians of the Southwest how to work silver, most frequently combined with the traditional turquoise. Today silver and turquoise, like the Navajo rug, are considered by most people to be traditional Indian crafts. Many Navajo did in fact become silversmiths, selling or trading their products to other Navajo. However, in the Nez Ch'ii area there have been no smiths for many years, and most jewelry is purchased from trading posts or from smiths elsewhere, particularly among the Pueblo people who practice the art much more intensively than the Navajo.

Both men and women wear jewelry—earrings, necklaces, bracelets, leather and silver wrist guards, rings, belt buckles and belts, and silver buttons and plaques sewn to clothing.

Jewelry is prized for its beautifying and decorative effect, but its primary function is as a repository and visible symbol of a person's wealth and status. Public occasions such as sheep dippings, brandings, Squaw Dances, rodeos, and so on are deemed proper occasions for the display of all the family's jewelry. Competitions or disputes between families is often marked by the sudden appearance of all the jewelry that can be mustered, and it is displayed on every occasion over a period of weeks until one or the other of the disputing parties ends the contest and tacitly admits defeat. Jewelry can be used to buy anything in exchanges between Navajo, but its primary economic function is to insure credit. All trading posts are also pawn shops and receive in pawn almost any item—saddles, guns, spurs, watches, boots, blankets—but the most common article of pawn is jewelry. Pawned for cash or to build a credit reserve to be drawn upon, especially during the winter, jewelry serves to meet economic emergencies and provide some buffer against the lean months of the winter. Most traders hold pawned jewelry long after the legal limit has expired, and many do not sell expired pawn belonging to regular customers without first asking if they intend to redeem the piece in question. When pawned jewelry is not redeemed, it is first displayed in the trader's store for sale to other Navajo or finally sold to large jewelry-buying firms, operating from Gallup, New Mexico, and from there transferred into the marketplace.

Thus, while jewelry generates a great deal of economic activity, it cannot really be considered a product of the area because it was first purchased from the outside before entering into the economics of Nez Ch'ii. In the past a person's jewelry was buried with him when he died. Rich men were often accused of grave robbery as an explanation of their good fortune. However, today most jewelry is passed on to offspring or siblings before the death of an old person so the family does not lose this important capital investment.

RITUAL TRADE

The Nez Ch'ii trading post stocks and displays several thousand items of food and merchandise. Of these, only some pieces of jewelry and rugs are of Navajo manufacture. There are, however, two other items of Indian origin regularly stocked by the trader as part of his traditional service to the community—buckskins and baskets.

Both the flat handwoven basket and the tanned buckskin are prized, often required payment in certain ritual contexts. The baskets, particularly, are required in the course of curing ceremonies and as part payment to the singer. In neither case is there any utilitarian or real commercial value attached to the items. To serve his customer, the trader keeps a number of baskets of varying size and quality and a number of buckskins on hand. He sells these at a standard price to Navajo, and usually the day after the ceremony buys them back from the singer's wife at a slightly lower price. The baskets and hides circulate and recirculate in the area, the trader earning a few dollars at every exchange. The baskets are usually acquired from the northwestern portion of the reservation where there are a number of "Navajoized" Paiute families that retain the art of basket weaving, which has, by and large, been abandoned by the Navajo. Buckskins occasionally are brought in by men who have been successful in hunting expeditions off-reservation. The hides, tanned by traditional methods, bring a good price at the trader's, but the appearance of a new hide in the system is very rare.

The Store

The pace of commerce in Nez Ch'ii is leisurely. Inside the high-ceilinged main salesroom of the Nez Ch'ii Mercantile Company, one or two White and several Indian clerks move from customer to customer waiting along the counter. Sitting directly in front of the "pawn room" on a high stool behind a glass display counter with the cash is the trader, supervising the issuance of credit, receiving payment of accounts, and evaluating rugs and jewelry for purchase or pawn. Behind him, the pawn room is festooned with thousands of items of turquoise jewelry, guns, saddles, hat bands, even an occasional bow and arrow set offered in pawn by an old man, and perhaps a medicine bundle pawned by a desperate singer. To serve an old customer and on the off chance a museum or collector might want such items the trader accepts them. The pawn room, in all traditional stores, is made solidly of rock and cement and entered through a safe vault door.

The Navajo does not hurry his shopping. The store is the focal point of the community; it is a place to chat with friends, catch up on the news, flirt with girls, or negotiate with the informal prostitutes who generally operate near the store. Here, too, he can contact the bootlegger and with a few friends buy some illegal wine for a drinking party in back of the trader's corrals. On days when people have other reasons to come to Nez Ch'ii, such as Tuesday when the doctor makes his weekly visit or on days when unemployment checks or federal wool-incentive payments arrive, the store is packed from eight in the morning until well after dark. The trader, who is also the postmaster, already knows which of his customers has received a check and has prepared his accounts in advance, attempting to settle outstanding debts and at the same time encumber remaining funds. Even in these times of pick-up trucks or automobiles, a trip to the store is seldom short. A half-day seems to be the least time one spends in chatting, bargaining, and buying, no matter how small the purchase.

CREDIT

Like most general stores in rural areas, the Nez Ch'ii Mercantile Company operates largely on credit. Goods are advanced against seasonal income, wool, rugs, lambs, and, increasingly, seasonal wage work. During much of the year very little cash changes hands over the counters of the trading post, and the trader virtually finances the social life of the region for much of the time. In a very real sense, the survival of the Navajo people depends on the willingness and ability of the trader to extend credit. His own credit operations are dominated by the willingness of large wholesale companies off-reservation to extend credit to him and by the surety that eventually his customers will pay their bills in cash or products.

At the same time, the trader must maintain a relationship with his customers that insures that once they have settled their accounts, they will continue to charge merchandise at his store. To this end he must conduct a continuous public relations campaign attuned to the tenor of Navajo life. Even the most heavily indebted Navajo must, in all probability, be given more credit to finance a sing or assist in financing a Squaw Dance or *Yeibeichai* dance. Certain products brought in by Indians and sold will be exchanged for cash, even though the seller has a large account outstanding. In some areas, rugs brought in are not charged against credit, although they are in Nez Ch'ii. The trader is also expected to make contributions in the form of extra food to families staging Squaw Dances. And when his other customers buy candy and fruit as gifts for the hosts of a Squaw Dance, a wise trader makes sure his clerks throw an extra measure into the bag. Ceremonial requirements also affect the trader's inventory in other ways. Skeins of colored wool are important as gifts and for the decoration of horses, wagons, and, in recent times, automobiles and trucks during the "race" on the first evening of a Squaw Dance. A trader caught short of wool not only misses many sales but seriously disturbs his customers.

IMPORTANCE OF TRUST

Since the turn of the century, at least, Navajo material and economic culture has been dependent on the trader. Until recently, each trader had by virtue of extended credit and isolation a virtual monopoly in this area. For some of these men, the temptation to exploit his often illiterate customers by holding them in debt peonage, issuing his own currency redeemable at his store only, manipulating accounts, and overcharging and underpaying, was too great to resist. Today, government and tribal regulations prohibit these practices, and the increasing education and sophistication of the Navajo limit the ability of the sharp dealer. However, most traders have been honest and responsible figures in Navajo life and have related to the Navajo not only as customers but also as clients. The trader too amenable to sharp practice or unable to adjust to the very special style of business expected by the Navajo found that his apparently secure monopolistic position was not as secure as it had seemed. The Navajo needed not any particular person as trader but rather the trading post itself, operating in an expected and accustomed manner. More than a few traders have gone bankrupt because the Navajo, preferring to make long trips to other stores or tighten their belts and do without, simply refused to do business with them. Faced with such a boycott, such traders had little to do save sell out at as little loss as possible and move to another field. The continued successes of the dozen or so old-line trading families on the reservation must be credited in large part to their willingness to accept and adjust to the Navajo style of life, which they often do not understand.

Just as the Navajo must feel a rather personal confidence in the trader, he also must feel trust in the trader's products. Building an inventory for a trading post is a far cry from the popular view of collecting shoddy and cheap merchandise to be palmed off on unsuspecting "natives." Rather, the Navajo is a hard-headed customer, stubbornly loyal to products that have served him well and generally suspicious of new products. In a largely illiterate population, familiar and unchanging labels are of great importance. Carnation and Pet brands of condensed milk are purchased even though other brands might be cheaper. In 1960 an attempt of a new milk company to introduce its products by pricing them far below the market tempted many traders to stock them in the hope that the low prices would bring in customers. Some of the low-priced milk still remains unpurchased on traders' shelves. High quality, able to stand up to the rough usage of Navajo life, is demanded of housewares, riding gear, boots, and tools. Shoddy material may be sold once, but seldom will it be purchased again, and a trader known for such merchandise will soon find his customers going elsewhere.

Agent of Change

Today, paved roads and motor vehicles have made it possible for the individual Navajo to shop by visiting other trading posts and stores in off-reservation towns. The trading post is increasingly becoming a counterpart of the off-reservation department store, with cash sales predominating. However, in Nez Ch'ii and other remote areas such as Shonto and Navajo Mountain, the trading post remains as the central feature of the economic life and the physical nexus of social interaction.

The trader has been the most effective agent of change among the Navajo, much to the chagrin of the missionary and government agent. However, his impact has been in the material and economic fields. His success, in all probability, rests on the fact that he has made no attempt to challenge basic Navajo beliefs and practices and has exerted no pressure against Navajo social organization. Even today, the Navajo tribe feels compelled to consult with the trader's associations when it plans large-scale or dramatic programs or actions that might affect the economic life of the reservation.

$$\boxed{10}$$

Headmen and Chairmen

ALTHOUGH WE HAVE frequently spoken of the Navajo Tribe, no such entity has ever existed until very recent times. Historically, the Navajo-speaking, and -living, people never belonged to a single political body. No institution in Navajo life transcended the authority of the homestead group; no man held authority on more than a local and transitory basis. There was no tribal council, no chief or high priest. All Navajo recognized a relationship among themselves of a higher and closer order than their relationship with anyone else. Beyond that, however, group decisions were most frequently made by the homestead or independent nuclear units. Only where the interests of two of these groups were in conflict was there need for outside intervention.

The *Na'tanii*

In each area, men of prestige and authority did, of course, exist, but the nature of Navajo life often fragmented such power. Thus a well-trained singer, by virtue of his knowledge, had authority in certain ritual contexts and might have been consulted at other times on matters of ritual. His opinion might or might not have had force in other matters, depending on his personality and the general esteem in which he was held by his neighbors. Similarly, a successful man with large herds and many children had certain power because of the economic forces he was able to muster and because his success might have suggested that his advice was worth hearing (on the other hand, it might have suggested that he had become wealthy because he was allied with witches or was a sharp dealer and too dishonest to be trusted). A man with knowledge of war making, trading, or hunting ritual, and a record of accomplishment in these areas would have been consulted or followed in these contexts and not in others. Generally speaking, each "outfit" tended to have one dominant member, usually but not invariably a man who by virtue of age, material success, a large family, some ritual knowledge, and

122

a winning or dominant personality served as both the guiding spirit among his relatives and their representative to the rest of the world. Similarly, each district tended to develop one or two such men, chosen for differing skills or knowledge, such as a "war" or "peace" leader as reported by Adams in the Shonto area. The Navajo name for these headmen is *na'tanii*, a word used today to describe the high-crowned, flat-brimmed western hat so often affected by prominent Navajo leaders.

The position of the *na'tanii* was never formal, and no man could claim the position by virtue of inheritance or even because he had been so considered in the past. The authority of the *na'tanii* rested entirely on the willingness of the people to listen to his advice and, of course, on his ability to influence the actions of others through the exercise of his material wealth and the manipulation of kinship relations.

In such a context there could, of course, be no crimes against the body politic or against the state. Rather, actions were seen either as violations of the natural order and thus threatening to the individual, his family, or the entire people or as torts, damaging acts committed by one person against another. Punishment for the first category was of course automatic and supernatural. For the second, negotiation between the interested parties or retaliation was the norm. If agreements could not be reached, appeals to public opinion and to the good offices of a respected leader or *na'tanii* might have been sought. His role would have been only as a conciliator, and failure to heed his advice was punished only by the mustering of public opinion against the recalcitrant party.

The following excerpt from my field diary illustrates this latter aspect of Navajo life today.

June 20

After the Square Dance, Agnes Beguey discovered that a turquoise necklace and a blanket had been stolen from her wagon. She began questioning possible witnesses and was told that John Three Mules had been seen in her wagon and that he had been drinking heavily. Agnes asked me if I would take her to find him. We called on his mother about five miles away and then on two or three other homesteads, failing to find him each time. On the fourth try, the homestead of the wife of one of John Three Mules' brothers, we found him sleeping off a terrible hangover. Agnes accused him of stealing her things. He readily admitted it and apologized, saying he was drunk and had run out of money and had stolen the things to sell and get money for more wine. He, in consultation with his brother, agreed to pay Agnes ten sheep for her loss. The agreement was repeated to the several relatives present, and Agnes got back in the car and left. The matter was clearly closed.

In earlier times when the Navajo country was much less heavily populated, certain *na'tanii* by virtue of records of success in war or in dealing with White men often wielded power over large parts of the region. Generally, in the prereservation and early reservation periods, it was these men with whom the government dealt and signed treaties or whom they provided with instructions to transmit to the Navajo. Often, the representatives of the government appeared not to have understood that these men had no power, in Navajo eyes, to commit their people to any course of action. The pre-Sumner history of treaties signed and treaties broken has been described before and is in large part a result of this failure to understand the true nature of Navajo political life. After 1870, when Indians became wards of the government and thus legally incompetents, the informality of Navajo political life became unimportant to the government. Navajo leaders served only as the means of transmitting orders to their people and hopefully as agents arguing for cooperation with the White men from *Waashingdon*. Leaders who urged resistance to federal programs or suggested independent Navajo action were an annoyance and were often ignored by the Bureau of Indian Affairs, while cooperative leaders not infrequently found themselves in favored economic positions.

The day-to-day life of the Navajo was largely unaffected, at least directly, by these problems. The Navajo being largely self-sufficient, living in remote and often inaccessible country and contacting the White world only through the agency of the trading post where he obtained the material goods he wanted, the informal rule of the *na'tanii* continued. Inasmuch as Indians were legally incompetent, the government had no need to consult the Navajo in matters such as transfer of lands, development of resources, location or management of schools, and so on. A small police force of Indians, usually veterans of the United States Army Indian Scouts, served to prevent such violations of federal laws that were applicable, as failure to send children to compulsory schools, and, less frequently, major crimes of violence.

The Tribal Council

When, in 1924, Congress declared that all American Indians were by virtue of their birth citizens of the United States, the situation changed dramatically, for the government if not for the Navajo. Decisions that heretofore had been made unilaterally by the Indian agent or the Bureau of Indian Affairs now had to be ratified by some person or some body legally representing the Navajo, who were now American citizens and no longer incompetent by definition.

This need led to the formation of the Navajo tribal council, which was first simply appointed from among leading and, generally, cooperative Navajo known to the Superintendent of the reservation.

This body served largely as a rubber stamp to ratify the decisions of the Bureau and its agents. To the Navajo, especially in Nez Ch'ii and other remote places, the tribal council, if the council was known at all, was simply a body of Navajo serving the interests of the White men in return for whatever material rewards they might receive.

The concept of representative government in which persons were empowered to commit others to action was entirely foreign to the Navajo and so was the idea of majority rule by vote. The idea that fifty-one people, for example, could decide what forty-nine dissenters must do was intolerable tyranny to the Navajo. Thus, for the most part the tribal council and tribal government had little real effect on the lives of the people of Nez Ch'ii.

The Growth of Self-Government

In the 1930s, however, after receiving a number of reports of the terrible economic and social conditions that existed on many Indian reservations, Congress passed the Indian Reorganization Act, designed to develop greater Indian participation in their own affairs and self-government on reservations.

Characteristically, the Navajo refused to participate in the Act, which they viewed as coercive (and which was indeed threatening to the favored position of the then existent tribal council). But, equally characteristically, the Navajo began in the 1930s and, with increasing momentum, in the 1940s and 1950s to develop their own unique government.

THE CHAPTER

An informal program, begun in the early part of the century and never very successful, of organizing "chapters" in each area of the reservation serves as the basis for the modern government. The reservation is divided into seventy-eight chapters, each with a secretary and other local officers and each electing a chapter delegate to sit on the tribal council. In addition, a Tribal Chairman and Vice-Chairman are elected by secret ballot on a tribe-wide basis. The council and the chairman administer an increasingly large part of tribal business and replace, or in some cases parallel, activities of the federal government. The tribe maintains a park service, a resources development program, and a highway department. Indigent Navajo are assisted by a tribal welfare program that supplements state and federal programs. Agricultural extension agents, formerly employed by the Bureau of Indian Affairs, have been replaced by Navajo hired by the tribe. Predator control and game conservation are under tribal direction. Hunting and fishing on the reservation are subject to tribal as well as state licensing. Except for major felonious crimes, tribal courts, presided over and staffed by Navajo, administer both civil and criminal justice. An increasingly efficient and dedicated tribal police force keeps the peace and enforces the law.

THE POLICE

In the case of tribal law enforcement and the administration of justice, the Navajo are making their own unique adaptations and adjustments. Viewing the police from a traditional viewpoint, the people of Nez Ch'ii tend to expect them to side with what public opinion considers the injured party. The fact that the policeman is a neutral in disputes between individuals is most resented, as is the refusal of the police to take immediate action when asked, for instance, to arbitrate a dispute between a Squaw Dance host and a medicine man over a point of ritual. At the same time, the idea of crimes against the public is still difficult to understand. Thus, in a case of assault the Navajo expect the injured party to be supported by the police, unless the attack was a matter of revenge, which then, of course, is not the business of the police.

Drunkenness and other violations of tribal law that do not do damage or injury to another individual are not viewed as crimes of any sort, and police action, which is most frequently encountered in this context, is bitterly resented. In general, the police, the tribal delegate, and the other activities of the tribal government in Window Rock are seen merely as extensions of the power of *Waashingdon*, and the agents of tribal government merely as Navajo carrying out the orders, or at least acting in the interests of, the Whites.

THE GRAZING COMMITTEE

One element of tribal government has begun to play an important and meaningful role in the affairs of Nez Ch'ii and has become completely institutionalized. In earlier times when population pressure was lighter, disputes between graziers over grass or water were seldom serious matters because it was easier to seek new pasturage than to fight for old. However, by the 1930s the population, both human and animal, had become so great that controls on grazing had to be established.

In the face of much bitterness and resistance, the government instituted a stock-reduction program as the first step in establishing a more productive livestock industry on the reservation. Along with the reduction program, the Bureau, in cooperation with the developing tribal government, instituted a program of range management that divided the reservation into districts corresponding roughly to natural divisions. Within the districts, each supervised by a Bureau husbandry expert, local Grazing Committees composed of local Navajo who were elected by secret ballot and in turn elected their own chairman were formed. The function of the committee was to supervise livestock operations, sheep and cattle dipping, branding, vaccination, castration of stallions and bulls, and the mediation of disputes between graziers in their district. Unlike the chapter system, which remained a foreign and intrusive element in Nez Ch'ii life, the Grazing Committee quickly became an institutionalized part of Navajo society. Members of the committee generally were respected members of the community, with many friends and relatives and a reputation for fairness and persuasiveness. Within their district, committeemen exercise considerable power inasmuch as they must approve movement of herds from one range to another, applications for loans, and changes in livestock operations, as well as maintain the records of livestock holdings, which in Nez Ch'ii are almost always in excess of the legal number permitted. However, there is little economic advantage in committee membership, and both the people and the member view it as an honor, a statement of confidence by one's neighbors. Perhaps because the authority of the committee is limited to livestock operations and reflects the traditional Navajo pattern of diffused and specific authority, the Grazing Committee has quickly been accepted. It provides a means of coping with modern problems of crowded ranges and livestock disease without violating basic Navajo values. And, as a respected singer or medicine man may be asked for advice and assistance in other areas of life, so are the members of the Grazing Committee consulted in livestock matters. Because they must deal directly with personnel from the tribal government and the Bureau of Indian Affairs, they are frequently sought out as intermediaries in matters other than grazing. On the other hand, the Bureau and the tribe often use the popular Grazing Committee members to recruit students for schools or announce tribal or government programs. To operate successfully, a committeeman must live in his community and be involved in the all-important livestock industry. As long as one member of the committee is able to speak English and deal with outsiders, the others have no need to, so that the most traditional of men may be selected.

THE RODEO

The people of Nez Ch'ii, as those in all other communities, encounter government on many levels. The Bureau of Indian Affairs administers many programs, including schools. The tribal government plays an increasingly important role directly from Window Rock and in the form of the chapter organization. The states supervise voting and driver licensing as well as brand registration and the recording of livestock sales. With the exception of the Grazing Committee, none of these governmental bodies has been fully accepted into Nez Ch'ii. On the other hand, there is a coherent political structure within which men of influence do affect community decisions and the activities of others. It does not find its focus in any of the specifically political institutions mentioned but rather in an entirely indigenous, although relatively new, activity—the Nez Ch'ii Annual Rodeo.

Two major forms of recreation, the mounted rabbit hunt and horse racing, have rapidly declined in popularity in the past years. They have been replaced by the rodeo as a primary interest of young men. The figure of the American cowboy has caught the Navajo fancy, and every young man aspires to be a "cowboy," that is, a person who performs in rodeos. Through the summer months rodeos are held in all parts of the reservation and today form the major secular activity of most communities.

A Navajo rodeo not only consists of the recognized rodeo events of bronc bull riding, bull dogging, calf and steer roping, but also not infrequently includes a horse race, perhaps a foot race, and usually gymkhana events such as barrel racing, which is a favorite contest for girls. In addition, a rodeo must include a "night performance" during which well-known singers, many of whom travel from performance to performance, deliver traditional songs. Not infrequently, teams dressed in traditional costumes perform dances and songs. The high point of the night performances are the exhibitions of hoop dancing, a vigorous solo dance borrowed from the Eastern Pueblos in which the dancer manipulates one or more hoops around his body. Young men who are adept in hoop dancing form a special class of performers who travel over the reservation displaying their skills; they are equipped with elaborate "Indian" costumes and accompanied by an entourage of supporters and admirers, much as a promising young boxer is treated in American cities. The rodeo and its attendant night performance are the annual responsibility of the Nez Ch'ii Rodeo Association, an organization formed entirely by the people of the community.

Although voluntary and ostensibly purely recreational in nature, the rodeo association is the nexus of political influence in the area. No one holding or aspiring to positions of political power or social prestige can afford not to cooperate with the planning or execution of the rodeo.

Chapter delegates from the three chapter areas in the Nez Ch'ii region vie for the honor of carrying the American flag in the opening procession. Often they must share the spotlight with traditional older men of the *na'tanii* mold who vigorously oppose all government or tribal programs. Members of the Grazing Committee all find a place on the staff of the rodeo in one or another capacity. The younger middle-aged and young men participate in at least one event, and others manage to busy themselves around the stock pens where the rodeo stock is held. Although the various agents and agencies of the federal government are ignored in the planning, the trader's role is clearly symbolized by his inclusion in rodeo activities. The trading post offers a prize for the outstanding performer; the trading post generator supplies power for floodlights and loudspeakers at the night performance, and the almost never otherwise violated rule of a 6 P.M. closing for the post is ignored. To enter the political life of the community an institution or individual must of necessity find its or his place within the structure of the rodeo.

Past and Present

In summary, the traditional political structure of Nez Ch'ii was one well suited to a sparsely settled, pastoral region. Each homestead group was in a sense an autonomous unit. Decisions affecting more than one such unit were made through negotiations, the operation of the principle of reciprocity and the mediation of informally selected headmen having little but admonitory authority. Authority itself was diffused through the population and was very specific in nature. In the past several decades a superstructure of political institutions, many of which are not fully accepted by the people, has been created to meet the current situation. However, the people of Nez Ch'ii have proven their ability to adapt and create or borrow new institutions to solve new problems. Gradually, often in a disguised form, modern governmental forms—representation, majority rule, and arbitrary authority—are becoming part of Nez Ch'ii life.

The basic problem is a transition from a system in which persons trusted individuals rather than institutions to one which is, in effect, quite the opposite. In the past, the individual knew which persons he could trust because of their ritual knowledge, their position in his kinship system, or their proven ability in face-to-face situations with which he had personal experience. Today he is asked to depend on such vague concepts as the law, justice, the tribal government, or the federal constitution. Because these are indistinct, and to him undefinable, he is distrustful and suspicious. Because these vague ideas have often worked to his detriment in the past or have not worked at all, he takes a position of, at best, watchful waiting for adequate performance. The same test of quality he has applied to material goods from non-Navajo sources he is now applying to ideas.

11

Change and Continuity

EVEN AS THE WRITER collected the information on which much of this book is based, the life of Nez Ch'ii changed. Within a single year the system based on the horse-drawn wagon became increasingly automotive in the wake of the area's first paved road running east toward Chinle. The trading store, which for forty years had sold wagons, added a service station and garage. The slight increase in expected tourist traffic motivated the building of a restaurant.

In five years permanently located rectangular houses, which were constructed with pitched roofs and made of logs or cement blocks, had replaced perhaps a quarter of the hogans that had existed in 1960. In addition, a new-style log hogan, nearly twice as large as the traditional-style one, had appeared; the larger size, which requires roofing of rafters and composition paper, is a response to the increased use of beds rather than sheepskins and blankets.

In 1960 many of the children had only begun to go to school. Many teen-age boys and girls were enrolled for the first time in accelerated programs. Today, most of the children of the area are enrolled in regular boarding-school programs.

In 1964, the Navajo, who had scarcely begun to accept political institutions four years before, registered in surprising numbers to vote in national elections. Two Navajo won seats in the New Mexico legislature. The latest campaign for tribal chairman took on much of the coloring of any election in America.

In the mid-1950s adherents of the Peyote religion, the Native American Church, were arrested. Others were stoned as witches by frightened and angry crowds. Today the Church is officially recognized, and perhaps a majority of the Nez Ch'ii population has attended Peyote ceremonies.*

The number of sheep grazing the district has dropped steadily, while the number of cattle has increased sharply and the number of goats swelled appreciably.

---

* See Aberle, 1968, for an excellent analysis of Navajo peyotism and its association with "relative deprivation" related to the stock-reduction program.

Persistence and Adaptability of Navajo Culture

Traditionalists among the Navajo and romantics among the non-Navajo decry the passing of the "old days." Yet, despite all the superficial changes and a number of seemingly basic changes of structure that have occurred, the people of Nez Ch'ii remain stubbornly Navajo.

For many tribal peoples, contact with modern Euro-American culture has resulted in social disorganization and collapse, loss of traditional values and language, and in many cases cultural extinction. For others, readjustment to the altered situation has resulted in the tribal peoples' finding accommodation in the new social situation on the lowest and most seriously deprived level of the new society. Yet others, to defend themselves and their values against the impact of foreigners, have made symbols of traditional material and social culture, and in a sense, insulated themselves against destructive change by refusing to change anything at all.

The Navajo are notable for their ability to adjust to new situations and benefit from the contact on one hand without losing their identity on the other. From the Pueblo peoples they learned of agriculture and weaving and borrowed numerous religious ideas and motifs that they put to their own uses in their own way. Equally profound was the change that occurred when the Navajo adopted livestock keeping as a basic economic activity. The changes effected as a consequence of animal husbandry were perhaps the most important inasmuch as the keeping of herds created new relationships to the environment that had to be recognized in social structure, personal behavior, and even values.

Despite these changes, the Navajo did not lose a sense of continuity and identity. Through several centuries of almost continuous contact with various foreign cultures, they have selected only those aspects of other cultures that fitted most easily into Navajo life.

Another element of Navajo reaction to the contact situation is a tendency to avoid intimate face-to-face encounters with foreigners. Previously, when interaction with foreigners was unavoidable, the Navajo almost invariably ritualized it, as they did with both trading and war in prereservation days, or used an agent between themselves and the outsider. Thus, the trader has been institutionalized by the Navajo precisely because he allows them to obtain the material items that they desire from off-reservation without the necessity of each Navajo's dealing individually with White society. The development of leaders in the past century followed these patterns, as men able to stand between the Navajo and the Whites became increasingly important.

Today, the problems faced by the people of Nez Ch'ii may not yield to the old pattern of aloofness. Non-Navajo culture impinges so incessantly that it is virtually impossible to remain unaffected. The increase of Navajo population has filled the reservation and made it impossible for the majority of the Navajo to make a living by traditional means. Radios, increased literacy, television in off-reservation boarding schools, motion pictures, and experiences in off-reservation employment have created new aspirations. The advantages of a truck over a wagon, a stove over an open fire, and electricity over firelight or lantern are seen by the Navajo. The old ways in material terms have no attraction for them as symbols of Navajo life.

Traditional culture such as that described for Nez Ch'ii remained viable and real until very recently, primarily because it was so well adapted to the natural environment of the Southwest. In many cases, adopting new ideas is impossible until new environments are made by such improvements as electricity, paved roads, adequate water supplies, and improved and available health services. Frequently, the backlog of desires and aspirations has to await the coming of these innovations before it can be expressed.

But there is a tendency to apply Navajo practices to new material contexts. Thus, it is commonplace to see a modern Navajo wearing a cowboy shirt and boots and perhaps even a plastic western hat and driving a powerful new pick-up truck with eagle-down tied to the rear-view mirror. Eagle-down was carried by Navajo runners to assure speed and endurance and was also used by horsemen. The same pride of ownership and display once expressed by keeping a large herd of horses is now found in assembling all the trucks and automobiles in a homestead group and arriving in a caravan to park near the trading post. More often than not, the Navajo will speak of his truck as *shiling*, "my horse."

Sources of Change

Although considered as extremely conservative by many Bureau of Indian Affairs administrators and missionaries, the Navajo have in fact proven quite amenable to change in material culture. However, the modern situation suggests the need for change far more profound than the substitution of one means of transport for another.

WORLD WAR II AND THE STOCK REDUCTION PROGRAM

World War II and the stock reduction program of the late 1930s and early 1940s constitute events as important as the Navajo stay in Fort Sumner in affecting the future course of Navajo history.

Subject to the draft and eligible to enlist, some thirty-five hundred Navajo served in the armed forces during World War II and were exposed to the experiences of learning new skills, living off-reservation, and associating with foreigners, as well as living and communicating for several years in English. In addition to the servicemen, an equal or larger number were recruited in West Coast war industries where they learned industrial skills, English, and the art of living with Anglos. Thousands of others worked in local defense work, the lumber industry and agriculture throughout the West, as these activities found themselves short of labor. Thus, perhaps as many as 20 percent of the Navajo people received their first experience with wage labor and jobs unassociated with husbandry. Moreover, they were introduced quite dramatically to the technical and material aspects of Anglo–American culture.

Stock reduction decreased the number of animals grazing on the reservation by more than half. More importantly, it drastically altered the relative distribution of livestock. Severe restrictions were placed on the number of animals that could be owned by a single person. This dramatically reduced the holdings of large grazers, many of whom owned over a thousand animals. For many Navajo, the impact was not so important because they owned small herds in the first place. However, those who existed by assisting well-to-do relatives were no longer needed in this role, nor could the small herder hope to achieve wealth through increasing the size of his herd to equal that of the rich. In overall effect it would appear that the reduction led to the creation of more, but smaller, herds. In most cases the number of animals permitted was too small to support a family, and at the same time the number of individual units being grazed made rational management of the range even more difficult.

The final consequence of the reduction was that it was no longer possible for a young Navajo man or woman to think of his or her future in the traditional terms of owning and caring for livestock and maintaining the traditional culture that was so well suited to this basic economic activity. For a young woman seeking a husband, a young man's ability to find wage work on- or off-reservation has gradually become more important than the number of sheep he may own. For young men, the need to seek wage labor has meant a rejection of sheep in favor of cattle because the latter animal does not require day-to-day attention. The dichotomy between men and women as a result of male involvement in raising sheep and cattle is becoming less marked. In the brandings of 1967 in Nez Ch'ii, many women and children were present as spectators, fine clothing and jewelry was worn, and the women took an active interest (but no part) in the work. Five years before, the brandings were considered a "men only" activity, and women seldom deigned to give cattle-work their attention.

WAGE WORK

The need for wage work has begun to create changes in Nez Ch'ii social structure. More and more often a young man takes his bride with him to set up housekeeping where he is working. If the work is intermittent, the couple may shift to traditional patterns and return to a cabin or hogan in the homestead of the woman's mother. But with permanent employment, the nuclear family tends to become more and more important.

TRIBAL AND FEDERAL GOVERNMENT

This tendency is reinforced by federal and tribal law, which recognizes the relationship of husband–wife and parent–child as paramount in matters of responsibility and inheritance. State laws that require that an unmarried woman file paternity and support suits against the presumed father of her child before being eligible for aid to dependent children stress the nuclear rather than the matrilineal extended family relationship. More and more frequently, matters of inheritance, paternity, and domestic problems are being taken to tribal courts for adjudication and less frequently to traditional *na'tanii* for advice. At the same time, men of the type that in the past would have eventually been considered *na'tanii* have developed into tribal judges or councilors who represent Navajo in tribal courts where non-Navajo lawyers are forbidden to appear.

More and more frequently the people of Nez Ch'ii find that they must turn to one or another agency of tribal government for the solution of problems that no longer yield to the traditional methods. Admitting that education is important in finding good jobs, the Navajo have in the past ten years reversed their indifference and become adamant that the treaty of 1868, which obligated the U.S. Government to provide one teacher for every thirty children, be honored. Building schools is beyond the capacities of the local Navajo community and requires dependence on the federal or tribal government. Similarly, water development and highway building are endeavors that cannot be solved in local reservation communities but only through the action of higher levels of government. As the tribal government becomes more complex, and as schools, hospitals, and other facilities become more numerous, more and more people from Nez Ch'ii are finding employment in the governmental structure. The demands of these new institutions require even more education, and already five hundred Navajo students are attending college on tribal scholarships, most of them training to be teachers.

However, much of what has become traditional in Navajo response to contact is to be seen in these new developments. It would probably be incorrect to say that the Navajo as a people are becoming more a part of Anglo–American society. On the contrary, most of the modern, tribe-wide political institutions that have developed in the past three decades are designed to assist the Navajo in solving twentieth-century problems without the necessity of assimilation into a foreign culture. As they become more modern, the Navajo are becoming, in their own eyes at least, more independent of the federal or state governments.

The logical conclusion of this development would be the development of a constitutional anomaly, an autonomous state within three states. It is doubtful that any such thing will ever happen. In the final analysis, the Navajo must develop a closer relationship to Anglo–American society as a whole. The pace of the changes described above is exceedingly uneven. Many of the people in Nez Ch'ii and other remote areas are scarcely aware of them. However, the reservation is no longer beyond the frontier of modern America. Paved roads cross and recross areas that a few years ago were accessible only on horseback. Electricity, telephones, radio, and in some areas television constantly present the outside world to Navajo eyes. School curricula, modeled on programs in the average American school, prepare young Navajo for easy communication with Anglo–American culture. The discovery of oil, uranium, natural gas, coal, and other minerals brings all the impact of modern economic institutions into direct contact with people who until recently saw only the trader. Programs to relieve the relative poverty in which many Navajo are forced to exist present the people with agencies of the government other than the Bureau of Indian Affairs. Growing political awareness has sensitized White politicians to the importance of the Navajo vote. It would be presumptuous to attempt to predict the final outcome of Navajo cultural change. For the immediate future at least, the Navajo will continue as an important element in the modern Southwest.

Navajo Power

In the ten years between 1961 and 1971 the pace of change on the reservation has increased. The Navajo, boasting now for the first time, not a few educated people, but many and of these a number with college degrees have become increasingly assertive. A separate junior college has been founded on the reservation and more and more Navajo people are becoming aware of the great discrepancies between their material and physical welfare and that of the American society as a whole. The cry 'Navajo Power' (Dine Bizeel) is being heard and seen on bumper stickers. The tourist oriented Indian celebrations in Gallup and Flagstaff are coming under criticism for exploiting Indian culture without directly benefiting Indian people. Other Navajo are organizing to protest the exploitation of coal deposits and the building of power plants which are polluting the air. The future which seemed so distant a decade ago, has arrived with bewildering suddenness.

References

ABERLE, DAVID F. "Navajo." In David M. Schneider and Kathleen Gough (Eds.), *Matrilineal Kinship.* Berkeley: University of California Press, 1961.
———. *The Peyote Religion among the Navaho.* Chicago: Aldine, 1968.
DOWNS, J. F. "Animal Husbandry in Navajo Society and Culture." *Anthropology,* Vol. 1, No. 1. University of California, 1964.
———. *The Two Worlds of the Washo.* Case Studies in Cultural Anthropology. New York: Holt, Rinehart and Winston, 1965.
FRANCISCAN FATHERS. *An Ethnological Dictionary of the Navajo Language.* Navajo Indian Mission, St. Michael's, Arizona, 1910.
KLUCKHOHN, CLYDE, AND DOROTHEA LEIGHTON. *The Navajo.* Cambridge, Mass.: Harvard University Press, 1946.
REICHARD, ALICE. *Navaho Religion.* Bollingen Series. New York: Pantheon, 1950.
SASAKI, TOM, AND JOHN ADAIR. "New Land To Farm." In E. H. Spicer (Ed.), *Human Problems in Technological Change.* New York: Russell Sage Foundation, 1952.
YOUNG, ROBERT. *The Navajo Yearbook.* Navajo Agency, Window Rock, Arizona, 1958.

Selected Additional Readings

ABERLE, DAVID F., 1961. (See References.)
A detailed examination of Navajo social structure.

ADAMS, W. Y. *Shonto: A Study of the Role of the Trader in a Modern Navaho Community.* Smithsonian Institute, Bureau of American Ethnology Bulletin, No. 188, Washington, D.C., 1963.
A detailed description of the trading business and the relation between the trader and the Navajo.

DYK, WALTER. *Son of Old Man Hat.* New York: Harcourt, 1938.
The autobiography of a Navajo beginning shortly after the return from Fort Sumner.

HILL, W. W. *Navajo Warfare.* Yale University Publications in Anthropology, No. 5. New Haven: Yale University Press, 1936a.

————. *The Agricultural and Hunting Methods of the Navajo Indians.* Yale University Publications in Anthropology, No. 18. New Haven: Yale University Press, 1936b.
Descriptions of traditional Navajo culture emphasizing ritual.

KLUCKHOHN, CLYDE, AND DOROTHEA LEIGHTON, 1946. (See References.)
Kluckhohn devoted much of his life to a study of the Navajo. A detailed survey of Navajo culture.

SHEPARDSON, MARY T. *Navajo Ways in Government.* American Anthropological Association Memoir No. 90, 1963.
An outstanding discussion of the institutionalization of modern political structure among the Navajo.

VOGT, EVON Z. *Navaho in American Indian Cultural Change.* Chicago: University of Chicago Press, 1961.
A discussion of culture change among the Navajo. An excellent review of Navajo prehistory and history.